MAP SKILL
Work Book

Social Science

Covering all the Maps of NCERT History & Geography along with Coverage of CBSE Examinations' Questions

MAP SKILL
Work Book

Social Science

Covering all the Maps of NCERT History & Geography along with Coverage of CBSE Examinations' Questions

CBSE

ARIHANT PRAKASHAN (School Division Series)

ARIHANT PRAKASHAN (School Division Series)
All Rights Reserved

ॐ **Administrative & Production Offices**

Regd. Office
'Ramchhaya' 4577/15, Agarwal Road, Darya Ganj, New Delhi -110002
Tele: 011- 47630600, 43518550; Fax: 011- 23280316

Head Office
Kalindi, TP Nagar, Meerut (UP) - 250002, Tel: 0121-7156203, 7156204

ॐ Sales & Support Offices
Agra, Ahmedabad, Bengaluru, Bareilly, Chennai, Delhi, Guwahati, Hyderabad, Jaipur, Jhansi, Kolkata, Lucknow, Nagpur & Pune

ॐ ISBN : 978-93-25790-41-4

ॐ Price : ₹99.00

PO No : TXT-XX-XXXXXXX-X-XX

Published by Arihant Publications (India) Ltd.

For further information about the books from Arihant,
log on to www.arihantbooks.com or email to info@arihantbooks.com

Follow us on    

Contents

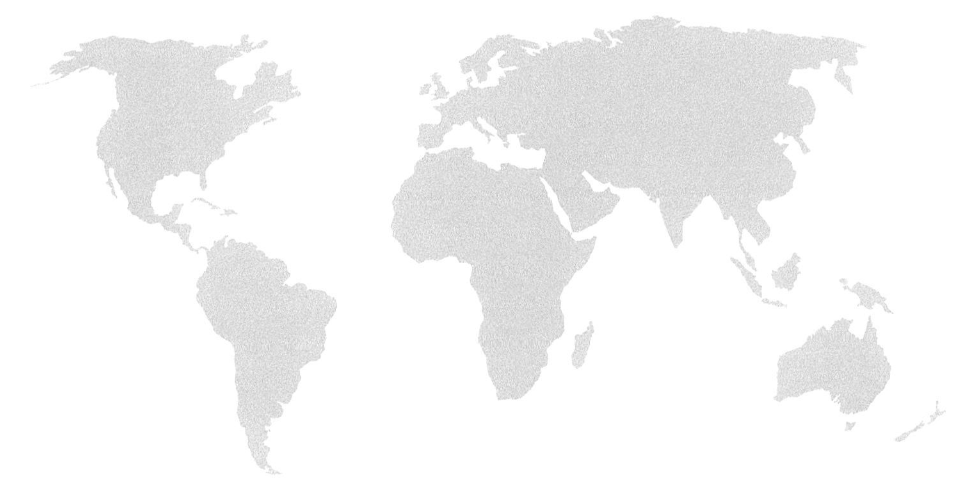

HISTORY

French Revolution:
Spread of Great Fear in France

(Chapter-1 French Revolution)

This map shows France and its divisions as they were in 1789. These regions were the focal point of the French Revolution.

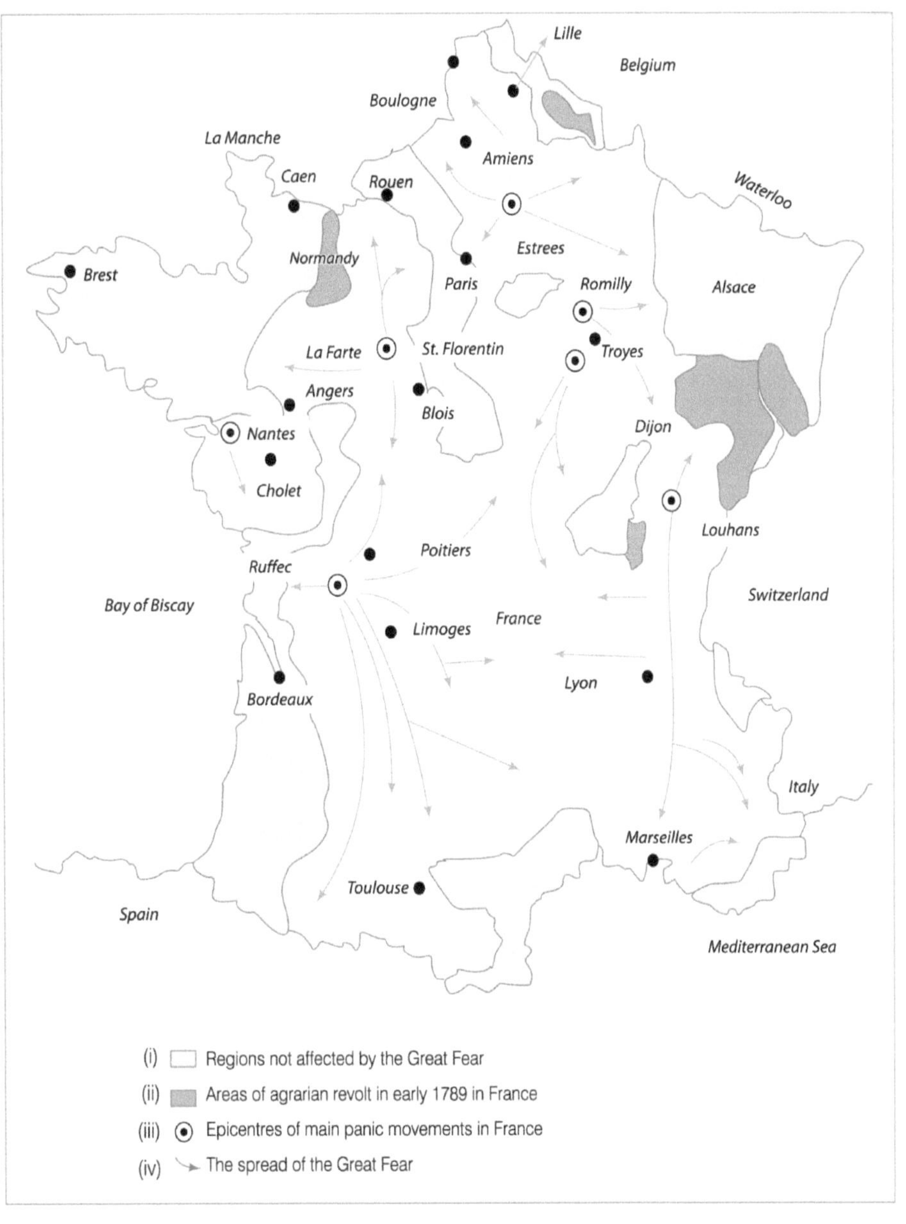

Practice Map 1

Q1 Locate and label the following items on the given map with appropriate symbols.

1. Identify (a) and (b) in the given map.
2. A Port of France related to Slave Trade
3. The port of France enriched due to Slave Trade

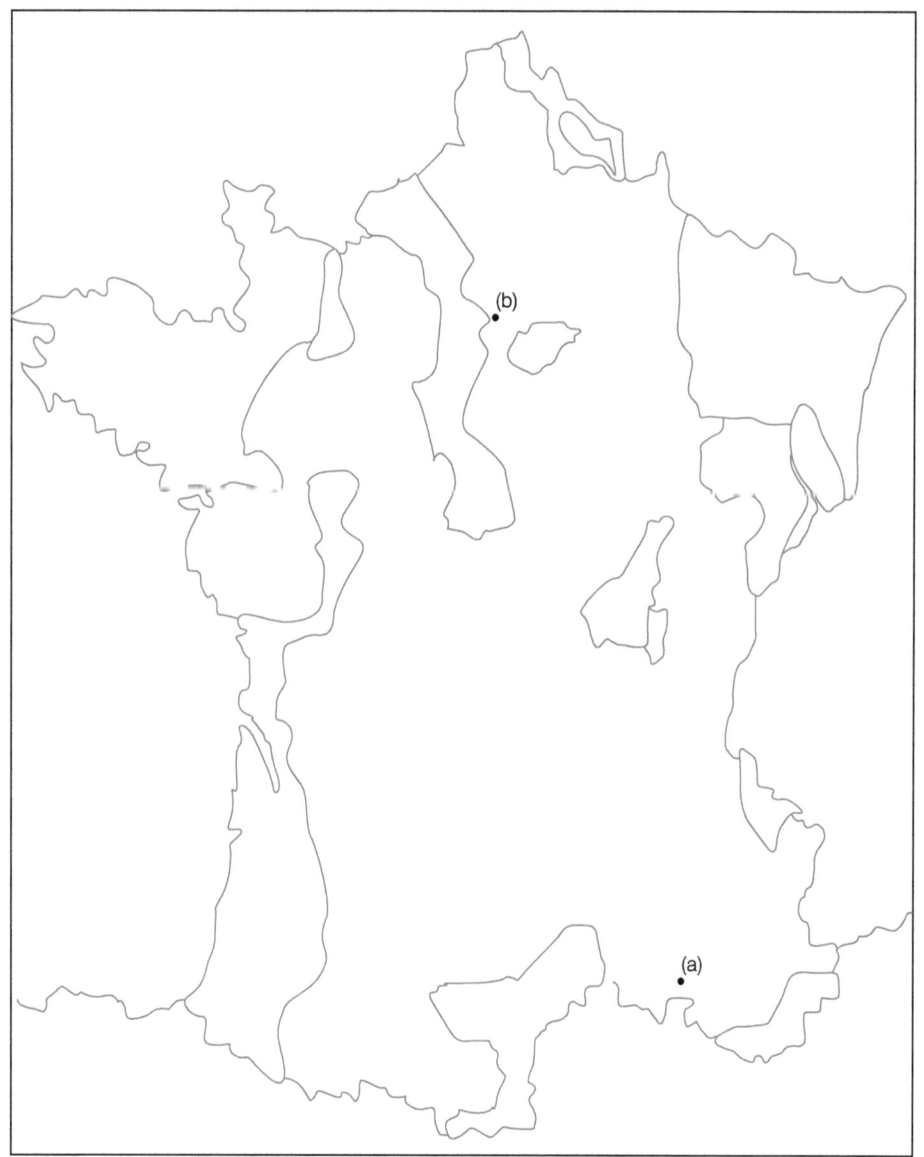

Major Countries of First World War
(Chapter-2 Socialism in Europe and the Russian Revolution)

Practice Map 2

 On the given outline map of world locate the countries that were central powers in the First World War.

Practice Map 3

Q3 On the given outline map of the world, four features are marked. These are the countries that were Allied Powers in the First World War. Identify them.

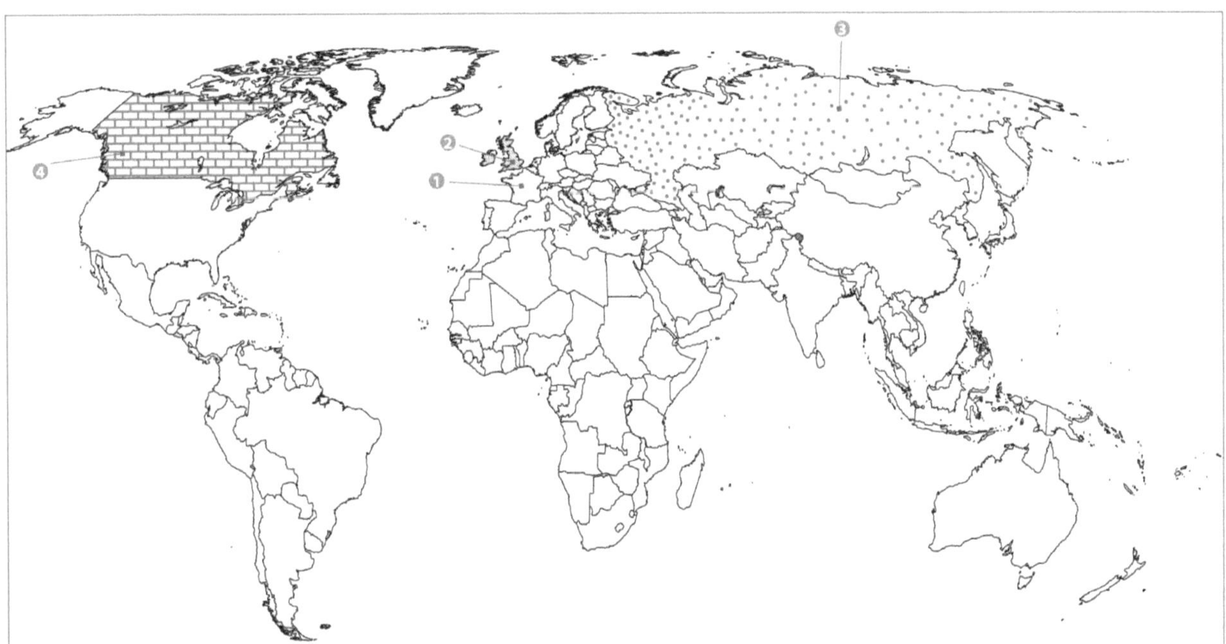

Major Countries of Second World War
(Chapter-3 Nazism and the Rise of Hitler)

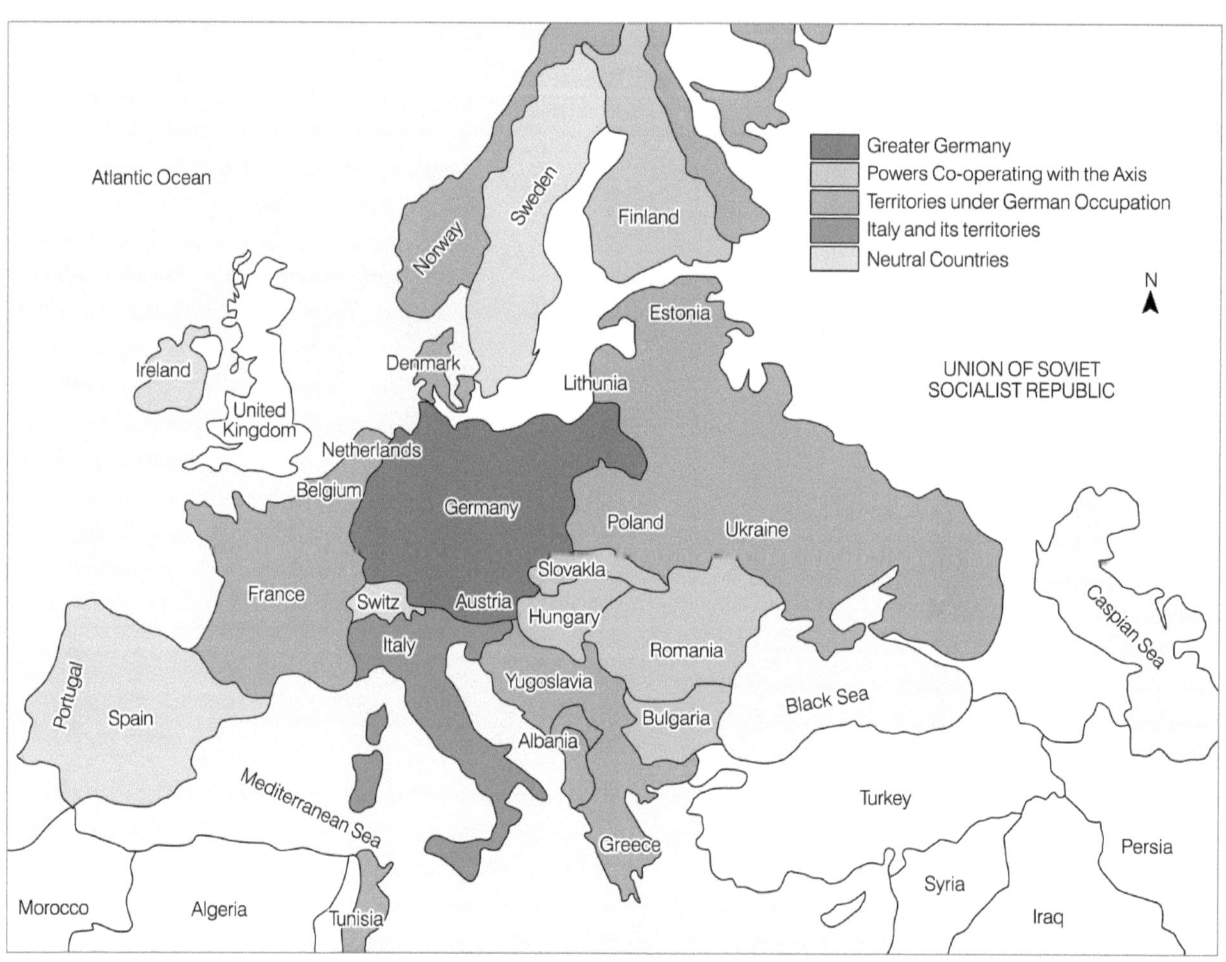

Practice Map 4

Q4 On the outline map of world, locate and label the countries that were Axis Powers in Second World War.

Practice Map 5

Q 5 On the given outline map of world locate the countries that were Allied Powers in the Second World War.

Practice Map 6

Q 6 On the outline map of Europe, certain features are marked. These are the countries that were once territories under German expansion. Identify them.

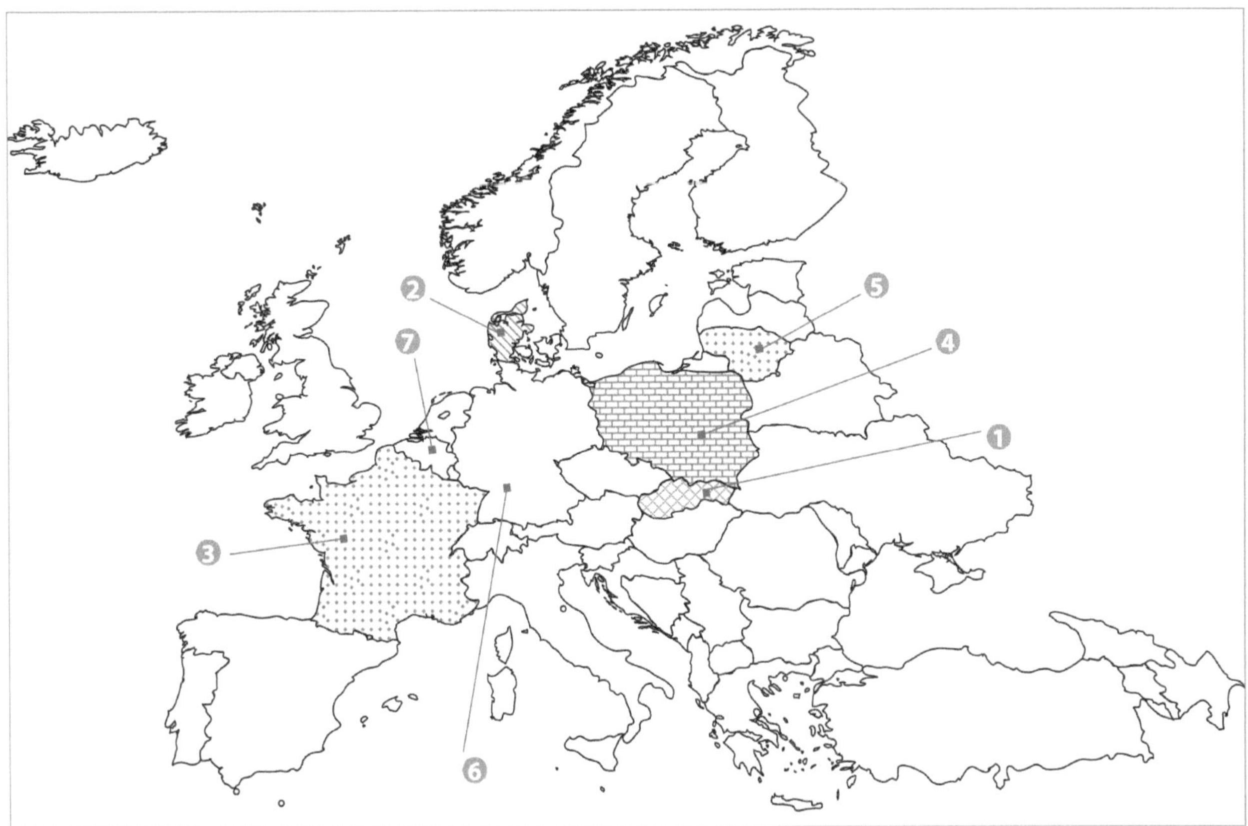

Map 1

Q1 On the given outline map of France, locate the following cities

    1. Bordeaux   2. Paris   3. Nantes

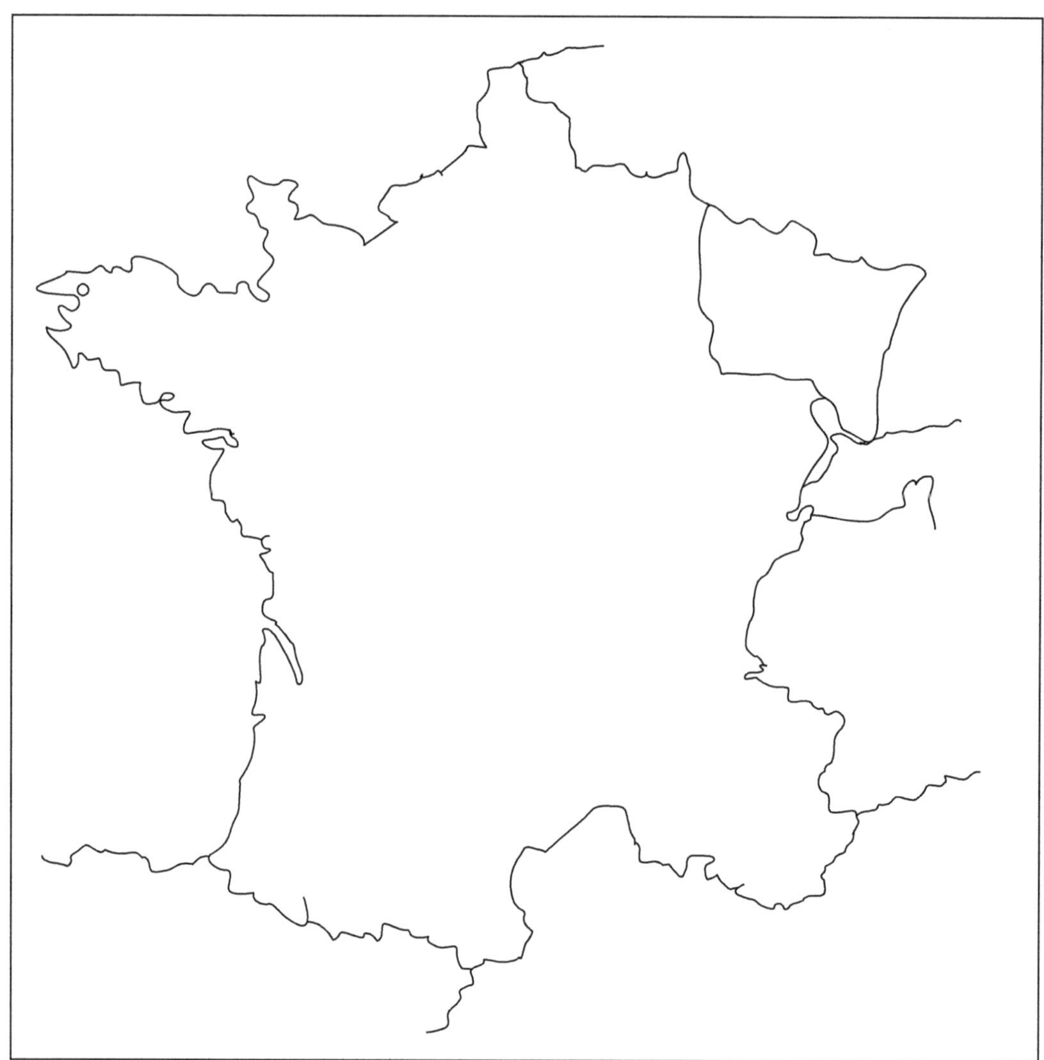

Map 2

Q 2 In the given outline map of the world, two features are marked. These are the countries that were Allied in the First World War. Identify them.

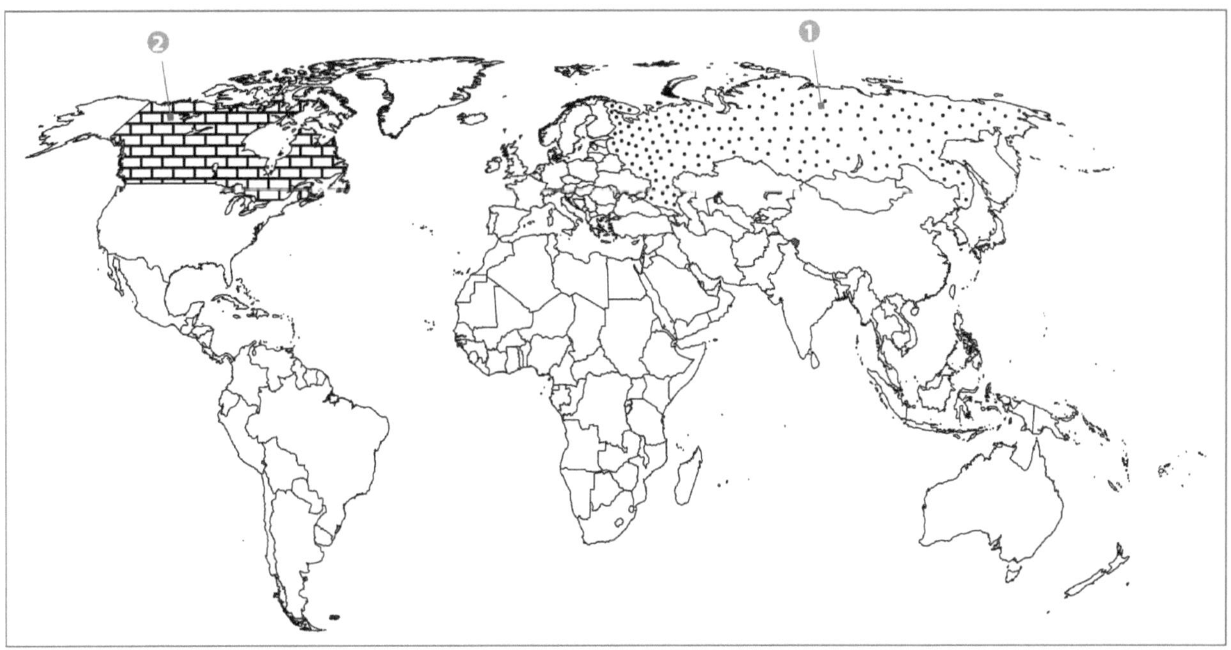

Map 3

Q 3 On the outline map of Europe, certain features are marked. These are the countries that were once territories under German expansion. Identify them.

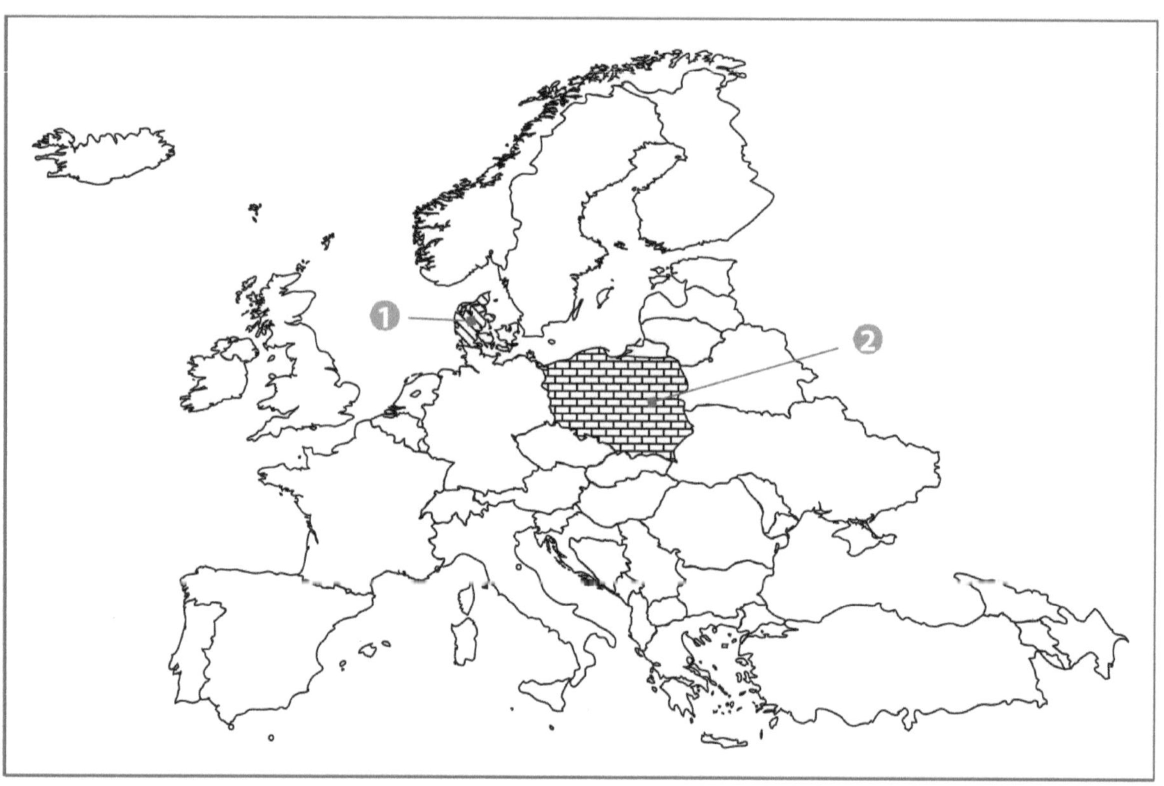

Answers (Practice Map)

Map 1

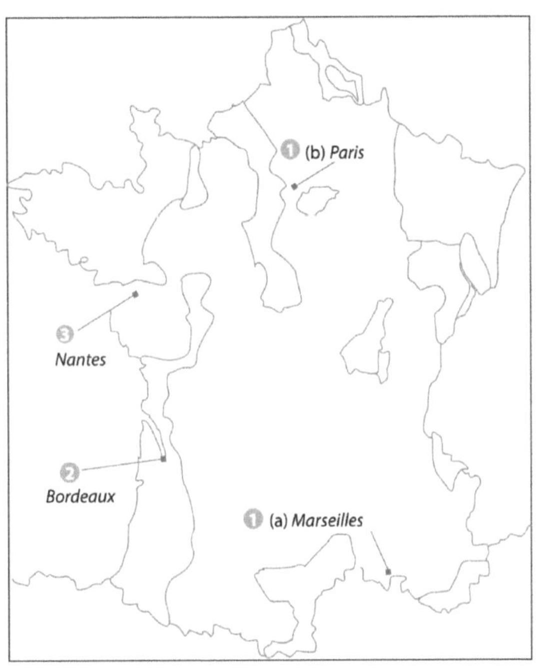

Map 2

Map 3

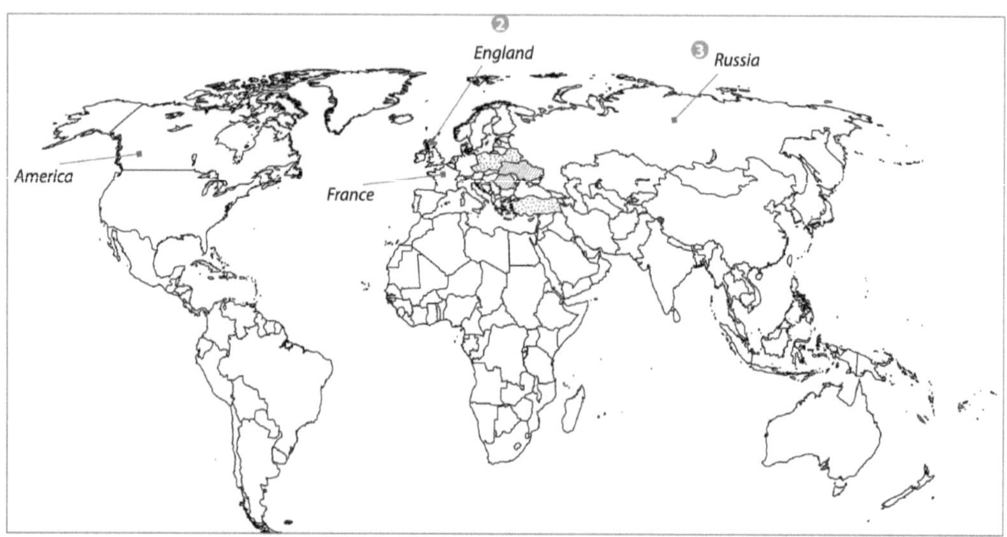

Map 4

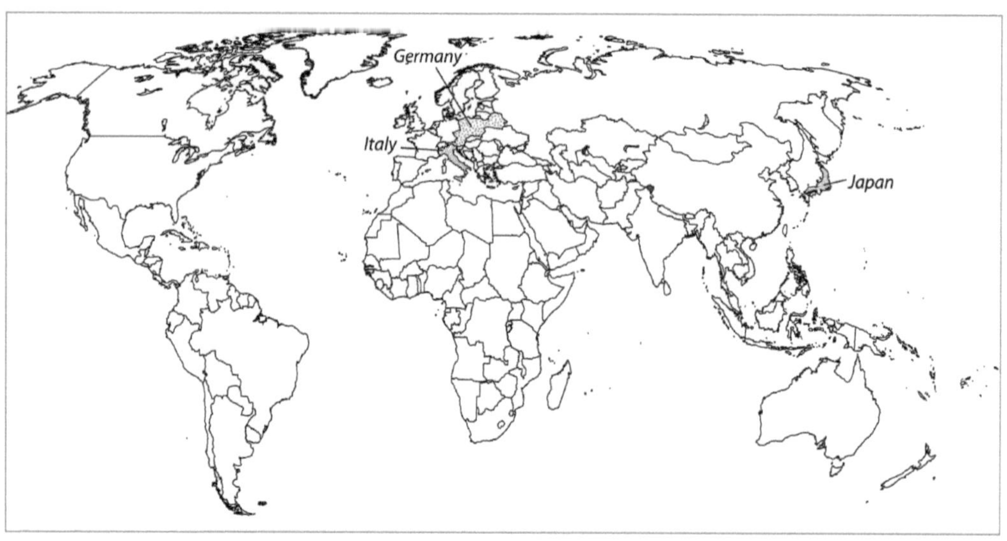

Map 5

USA
UK
Former USSR
France

Map 6

Denmark
Poland
Lithuania
Czechoslovakia or Slovakia
Belgium
France
Austria

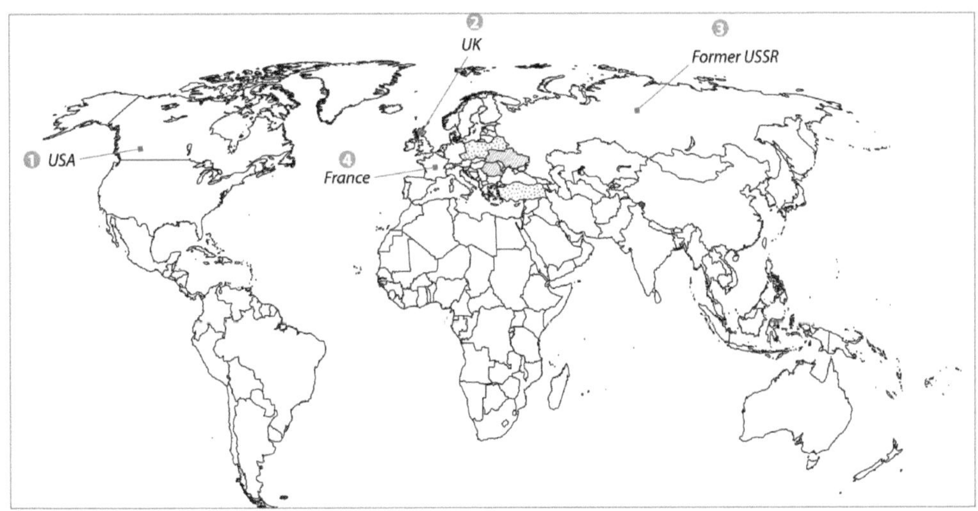

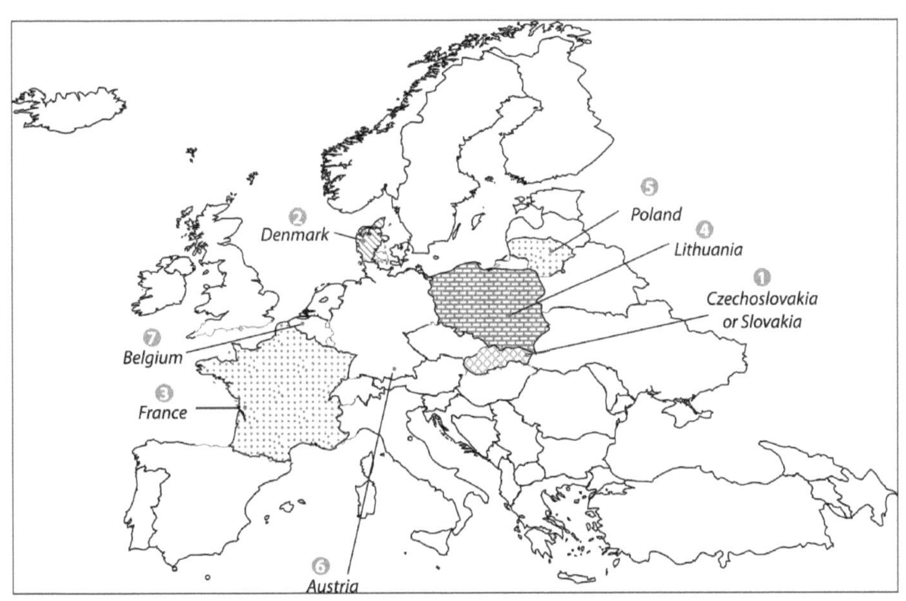

Answers (Exam Practice)

Map 1

Map 2

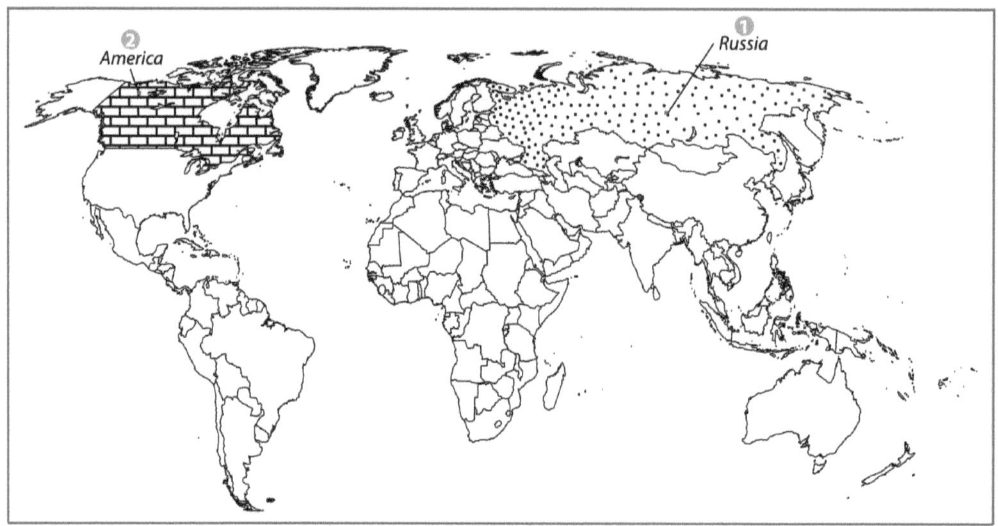

 Map Skill for Class IX

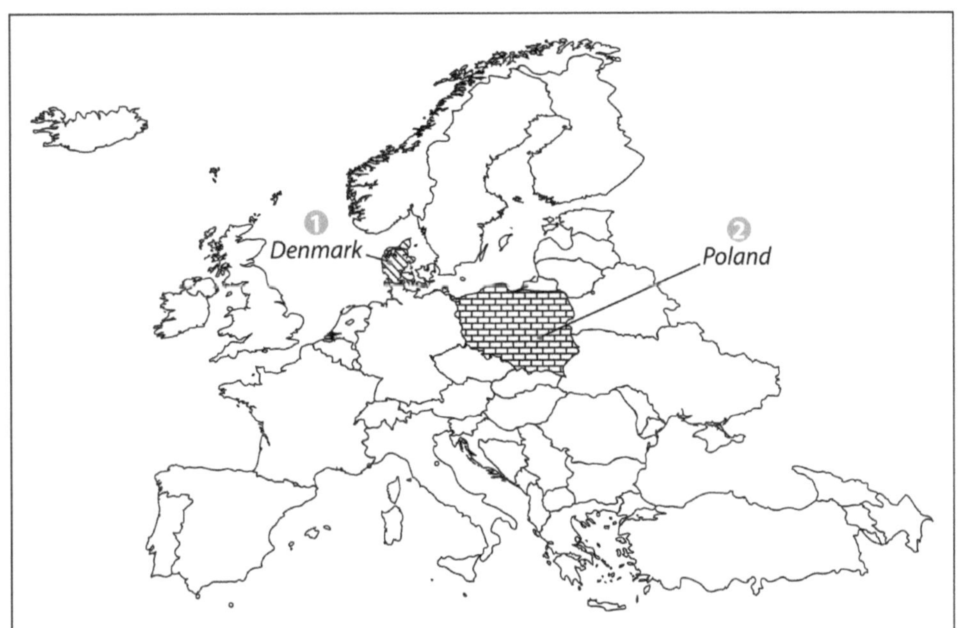

Denmark
Poland

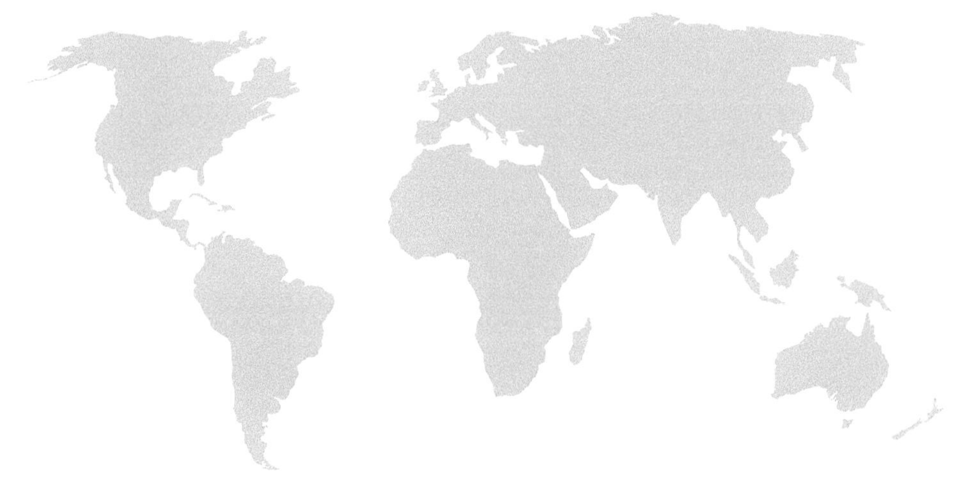

GEOGRAPHY

INDIA : Political Map
(Chapter-1 India-Size and Location)

The Political Map of India shows all the States and Union Territories. Presently, India has 28 States and 8 Union Territories.

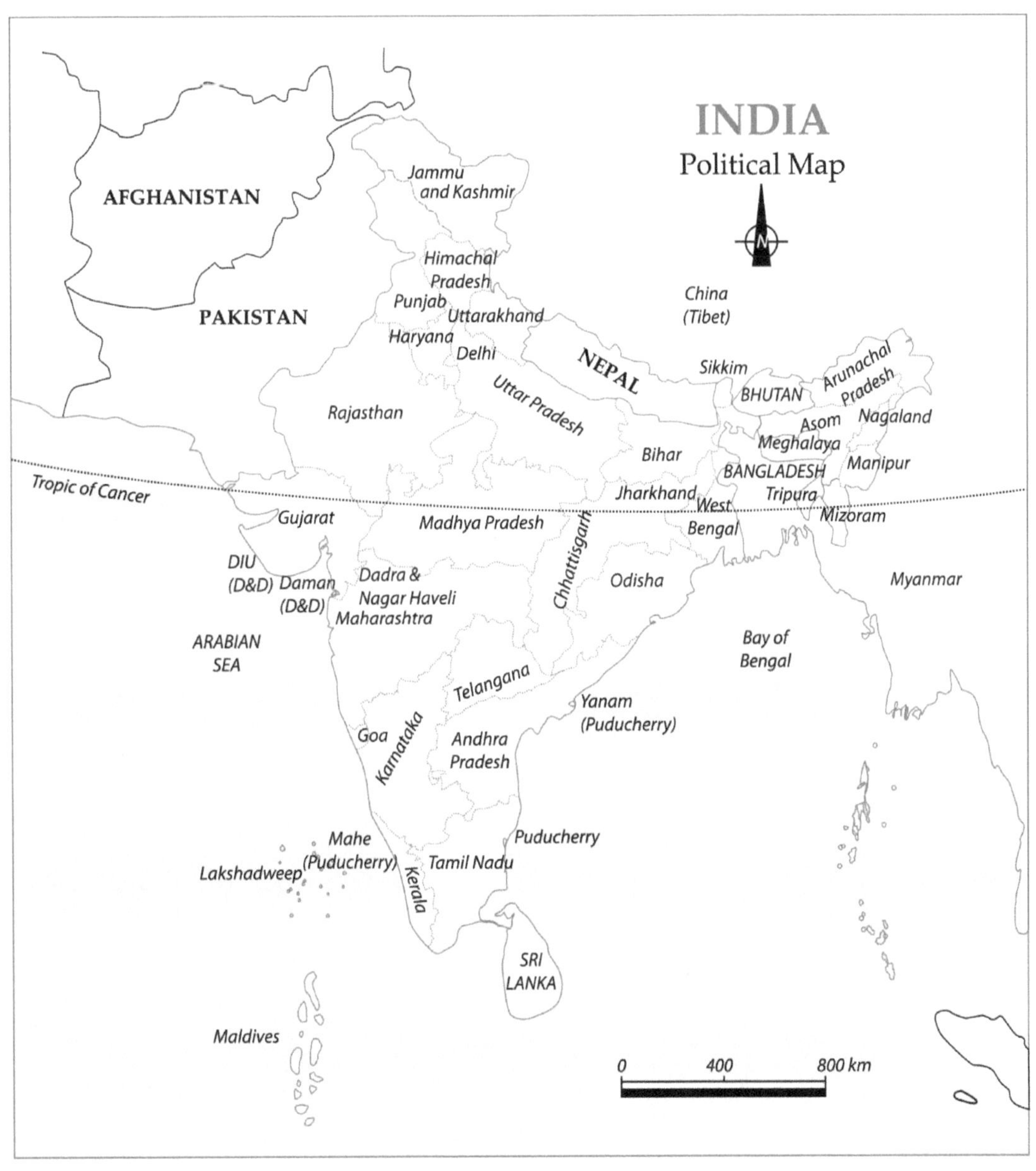

Practice Map 1

1 Capital of Uttarakhand
2 Capital of Assam
3 Capital of Madhya Pradesh
4 Capital of Tamil Nadu
5 Capital of India
6 Capital of Karnataka
7 Capital of Rajasthan
8 Capital of Gujarat

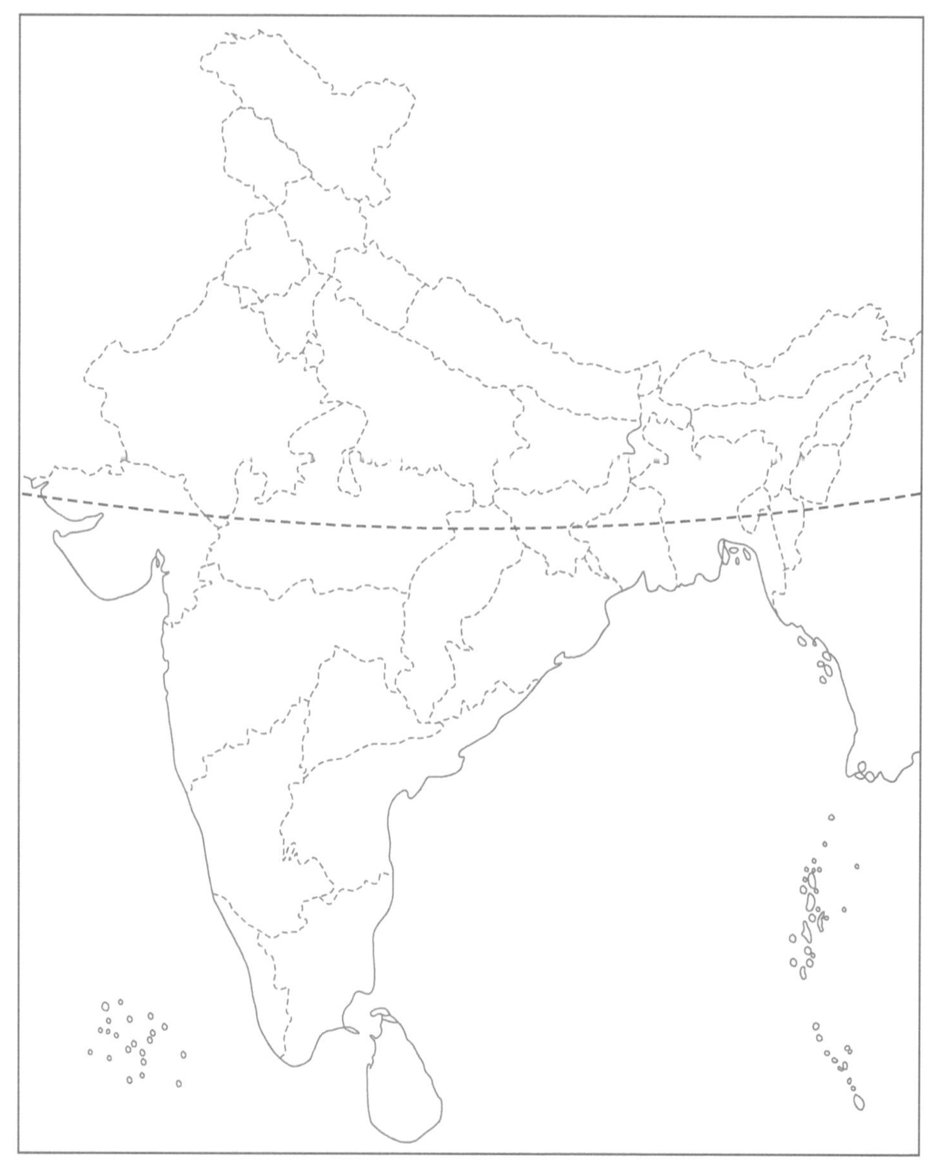

INDIA : Standard Meridian
(Chapter-1 India-Size and Location)

This map shows the important geographical lines which pass through India. These are Standard Meridian and Tropic of cancer. This map also shows the Eastern, Western, Northern and Southern point of India.

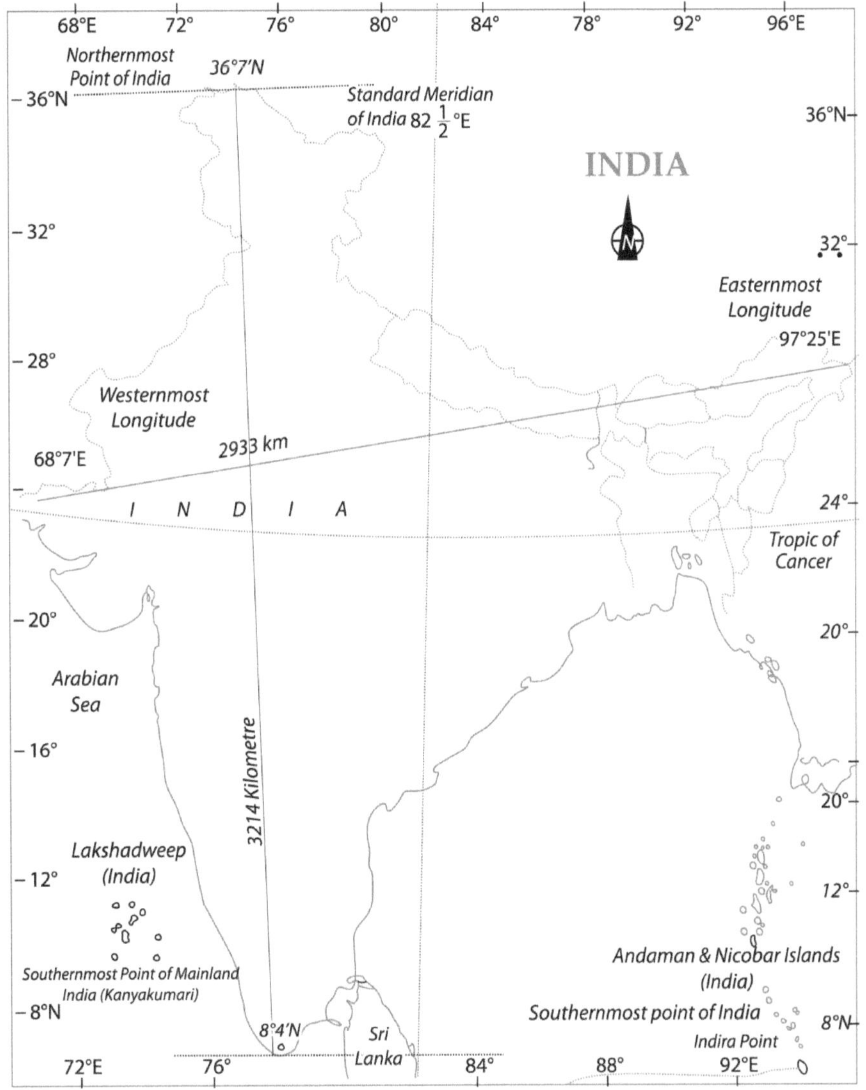

Tropic of Cancer passes through 8 states of India : Gujarat, Rajasthan, Madhya Pradesh, Chhattisgarh, Jharkhand, West Bengal, Tripura and Mizoram. Standard Meridian of India $\left(82\frac{1}{2}°\,E\right)$ passes through Uttar Pradesh, Madhya Pradesh, Chhattisgarh, Odisha and Andhra Pradesh.

Practice Map 2

Q2 Locate and label the following items on the given map

1 Tropic of Cancer
2 Standard Meridian

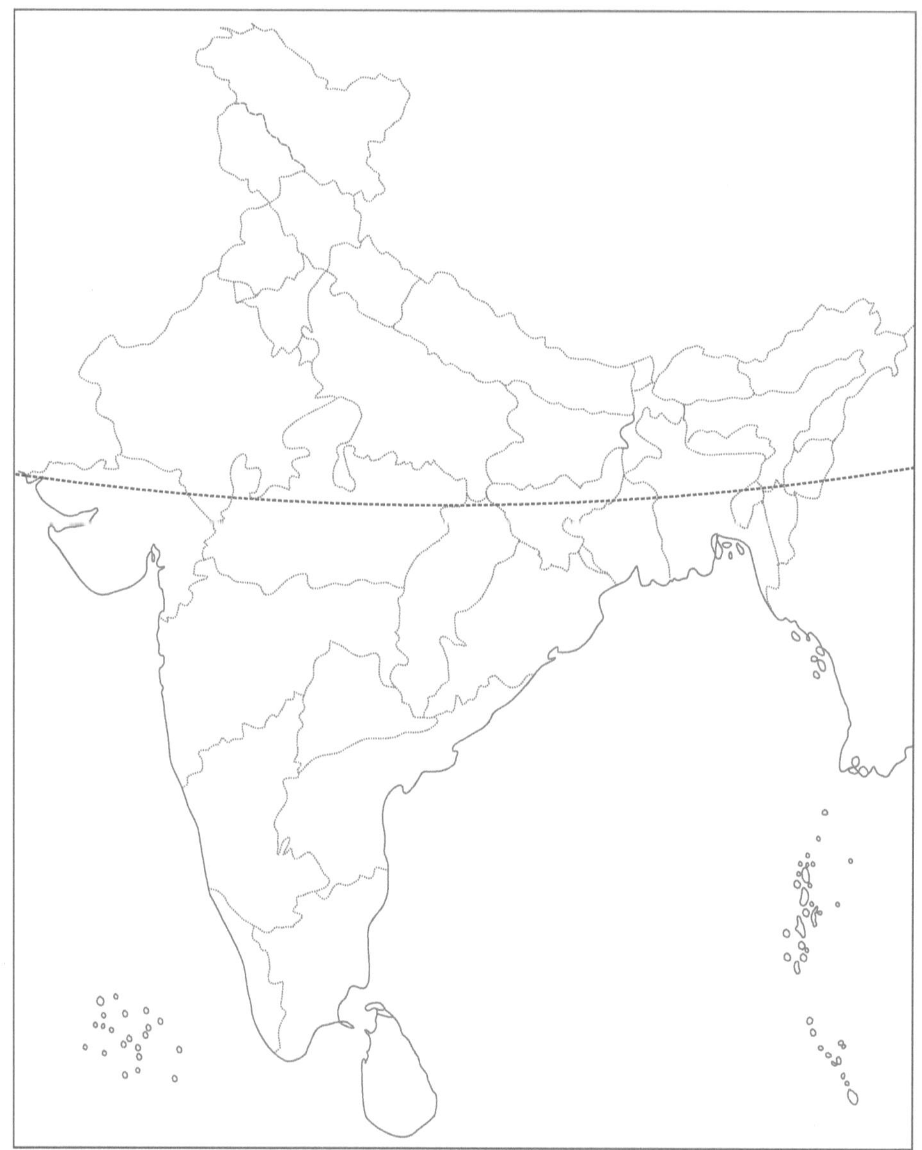

INDIA : Physical Features
(Chapter-2 Physical Features of India)

This is a physical map of India showing all the physiographic regions of the nation. In terms of physiography, the nation can be split into the following areas:

- The Islands
- The Great Indian Desert
- Coastal plains
- Northern plains
- The Peninsular plateau
- The Himalayan mountains

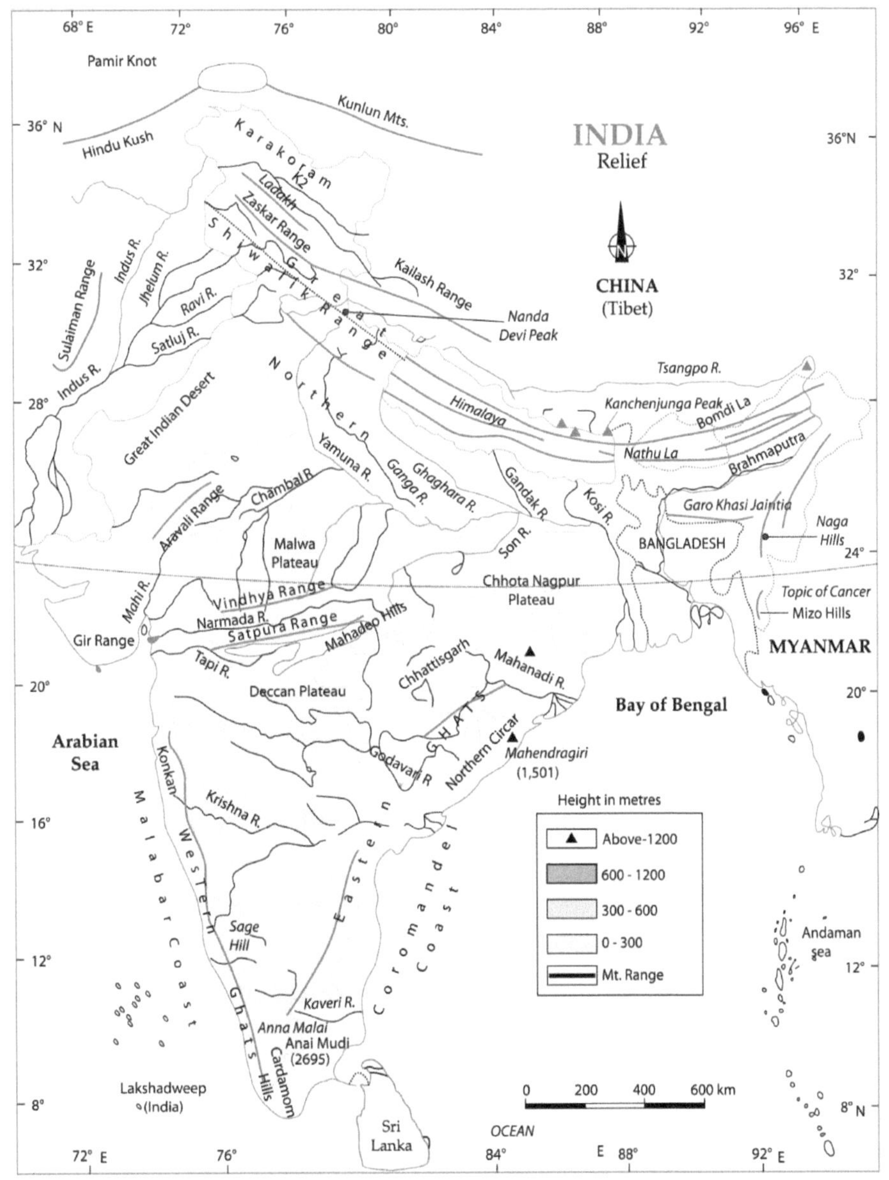

Practice Map 3

Q3 Three features are shown on the outline map of India. Identify these features and write their names on the lines marked on the map.

1   A mountain range between the Narmada and Tapi rivers.

2   The highest peak in the Cardamom hills.

3   A mountain range North of the Satpura range.

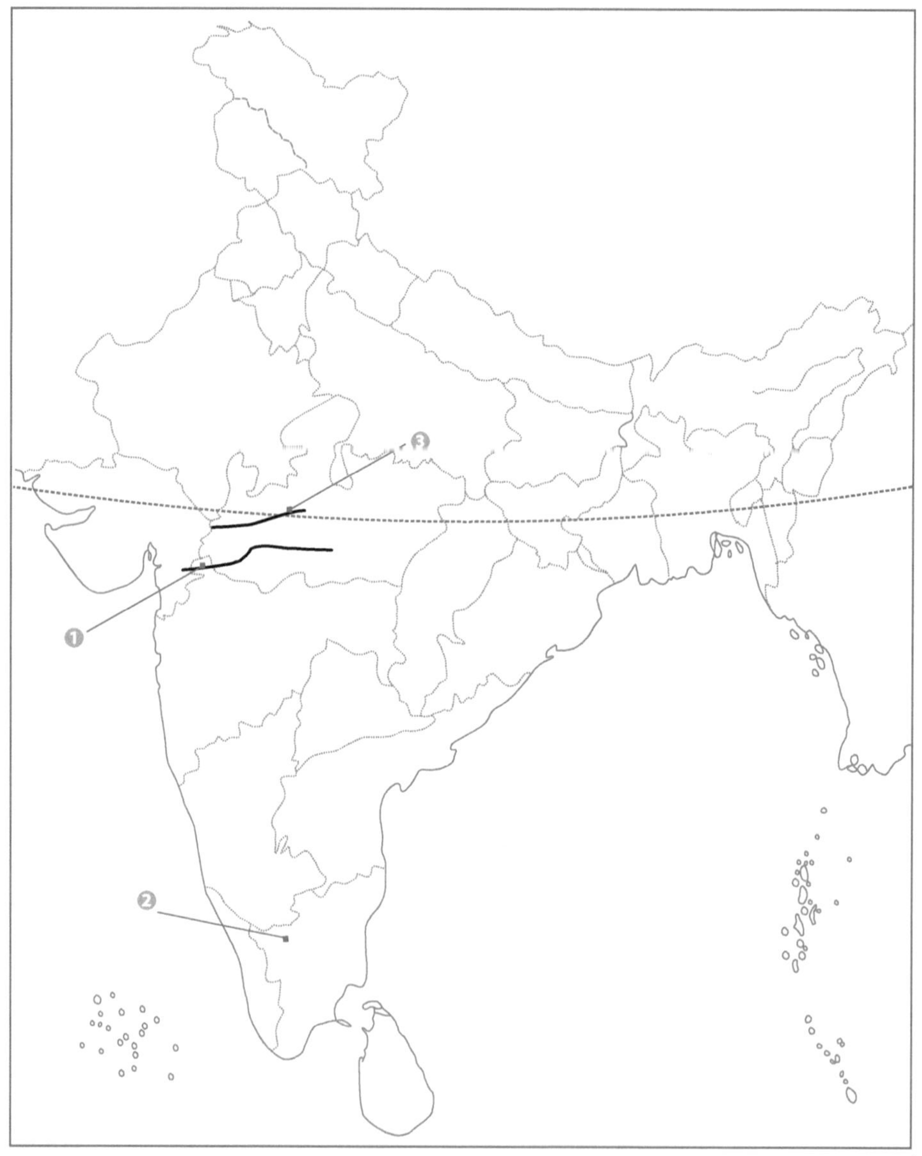

Practice Map 4

Q4 On the map, locate and label the following with appropriate symbols.

1 A mountain range lying mostly in Rajasthan.

2 A plateau lying mostly in Jharkhand and Chhattisgarh.

3 A plateau in West-Central India.

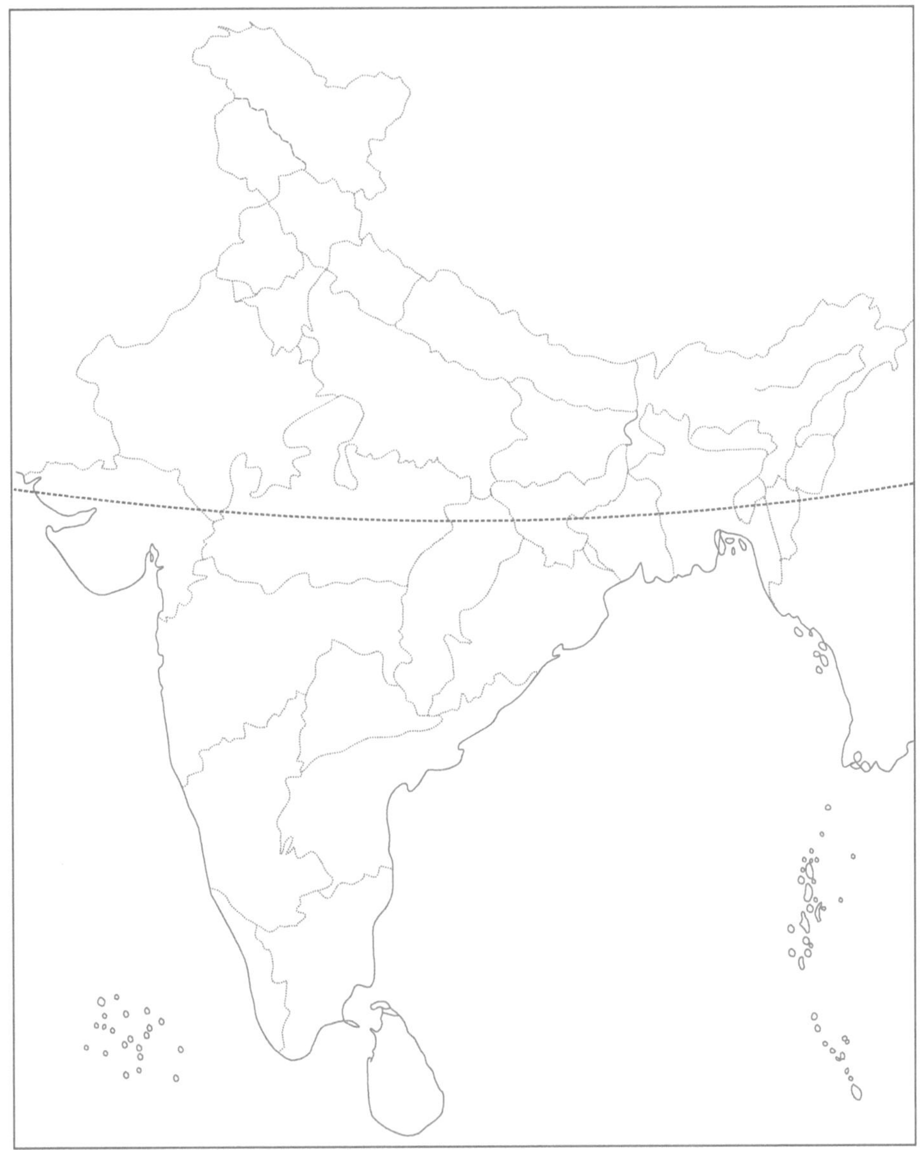

Practice Map 5

Q5 Three features are shown on the outline map of India. Identify these features and write their names on the lines marked on the map.

   1 A mountain range in Uttarakhand.

   2 The highest peak in the Himalayas in India.

   3 Ghats lie on the Western part of the Deccan Plateau

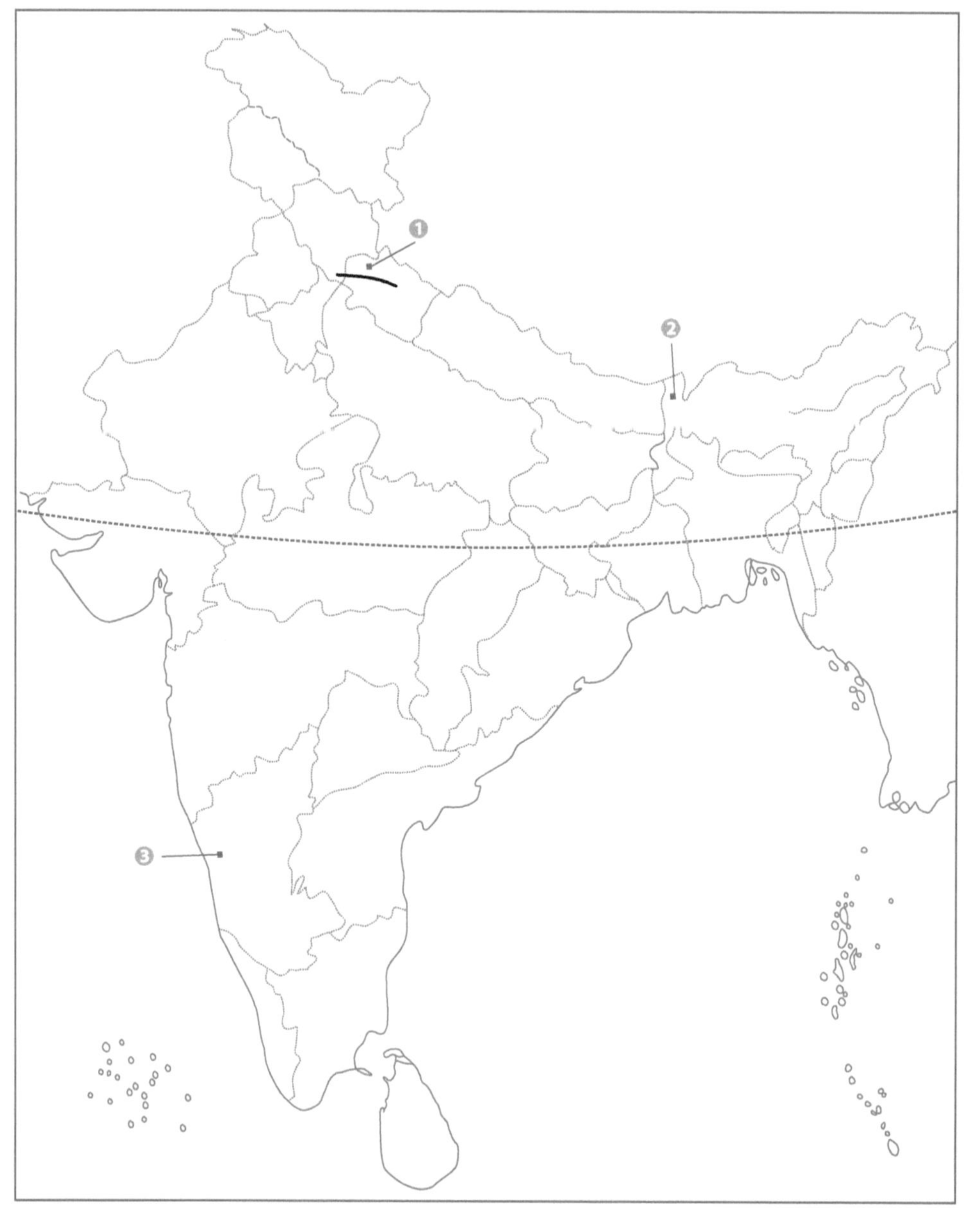

Practice Map 6

Q6 On the map, locate and label the following with appropriate symbols.

1. A region of the Peninsular plateau which is triangular in shape.
2. K2 Mountain Peak
3. Ghats lie on the Eastern part of the Deccan Plateau.

Practice Map 7

Q7 On outline map of India locate and label the following features with appropriate symbols.

1. Konkan Coast
2. Coromandel Coast
3. Malabar Coast
4. Northern Circar
5. The Karakoram Range
6. Zaskar Range

INDIA : Drainage and Lakes
(Chapter-3 Drainage)

This map shows various rivers that flow across the states, national capital, union territories and international boundaries. It also shows the major lakes of India.

Practice Map 8

Q8 Locate and label the following items on the given map

  1 Pulicat   **2** Sambhar   **3** Wular   **4** Chilika

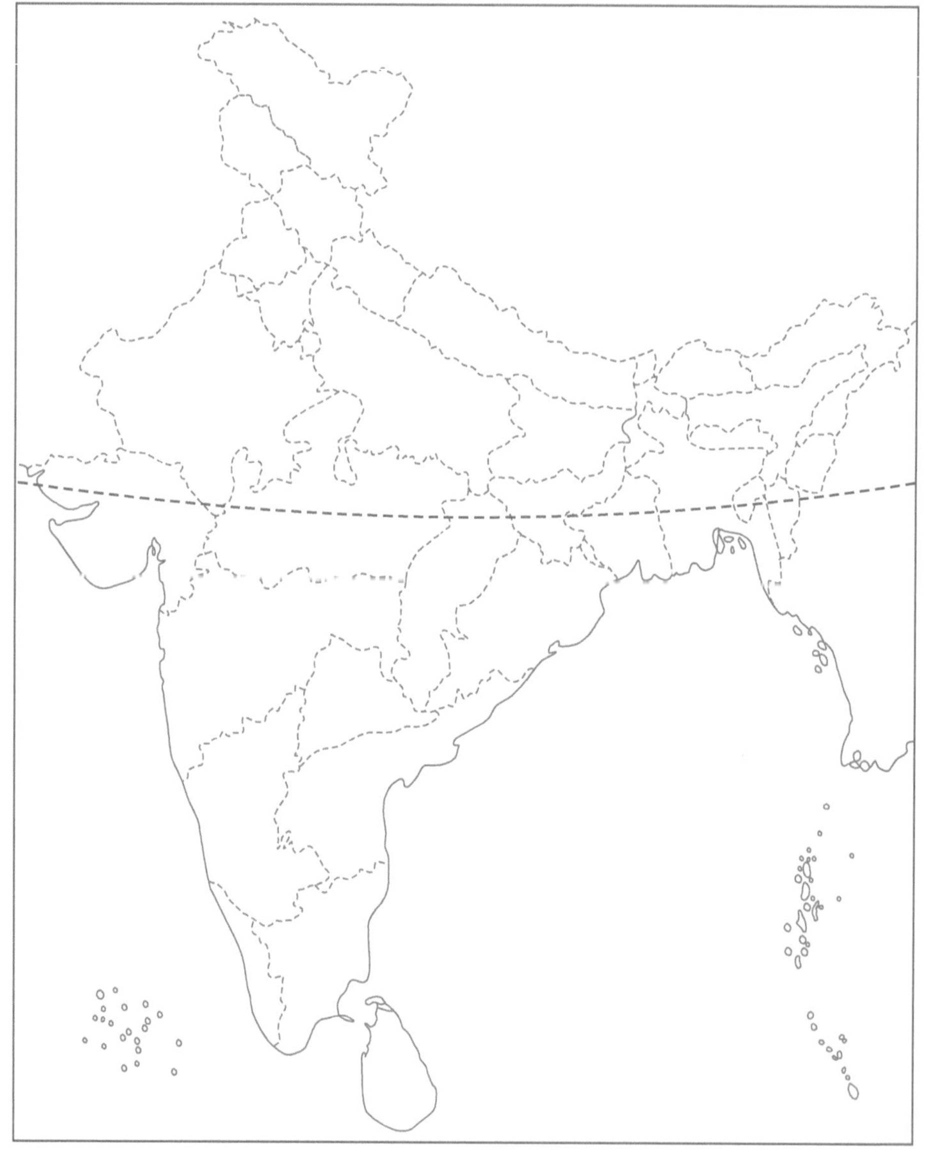

Practice Map 9

Q9 Identify the following Himalayan rivers on the given map

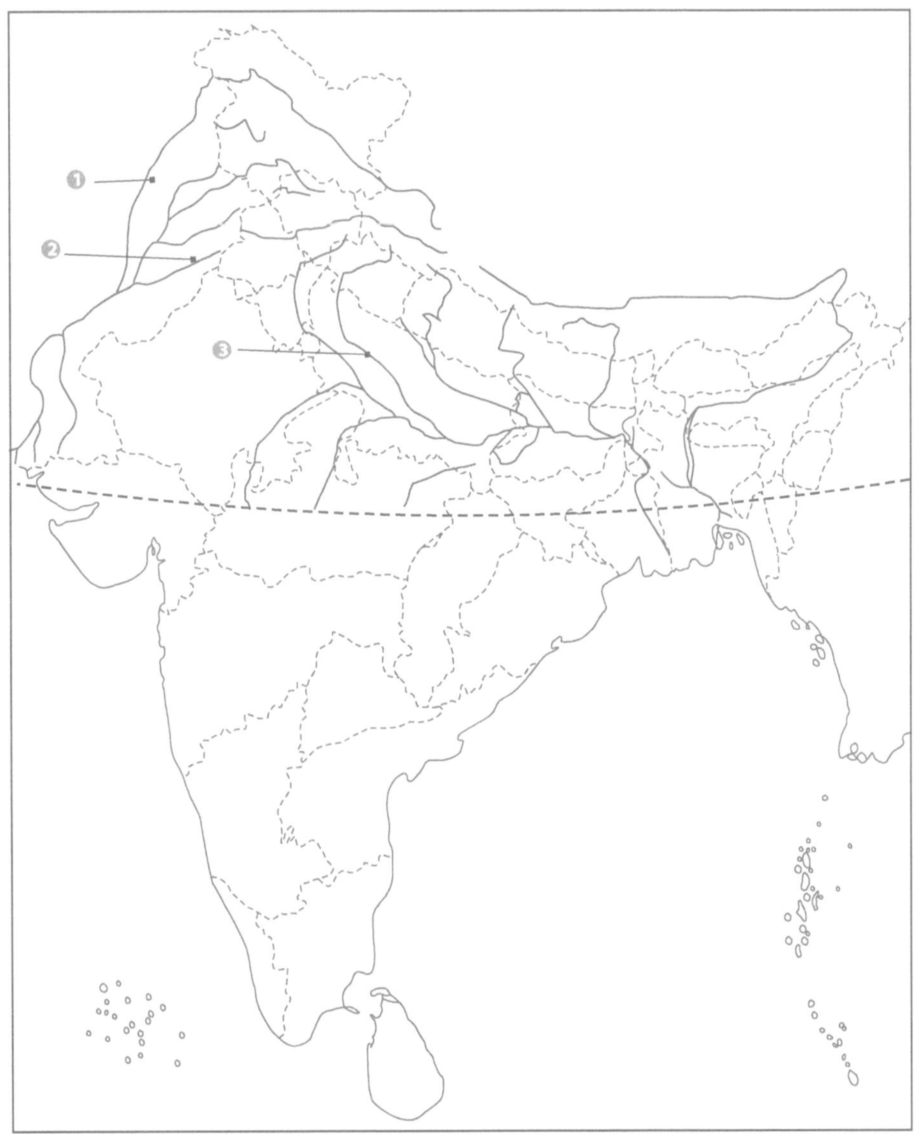

Practice Map 10

 Identify the following Peninsular rivers on the given map

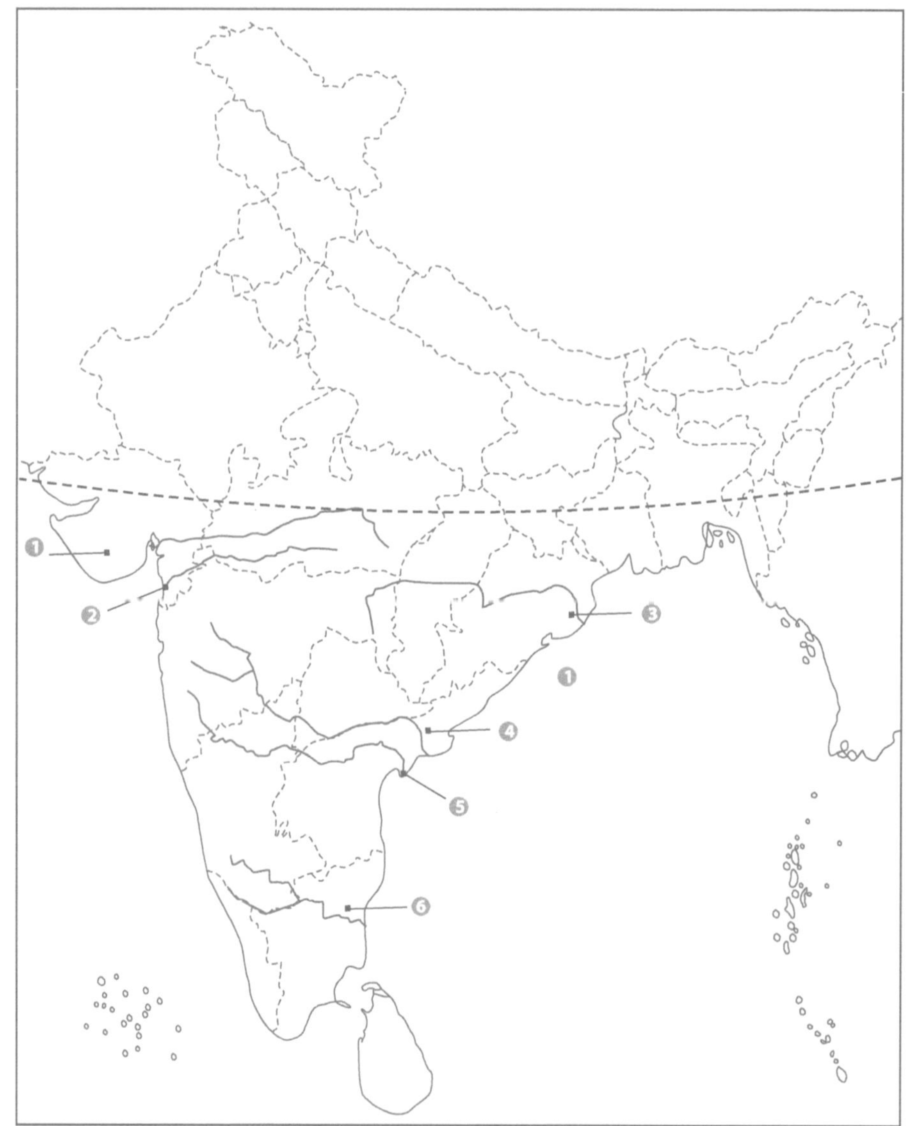

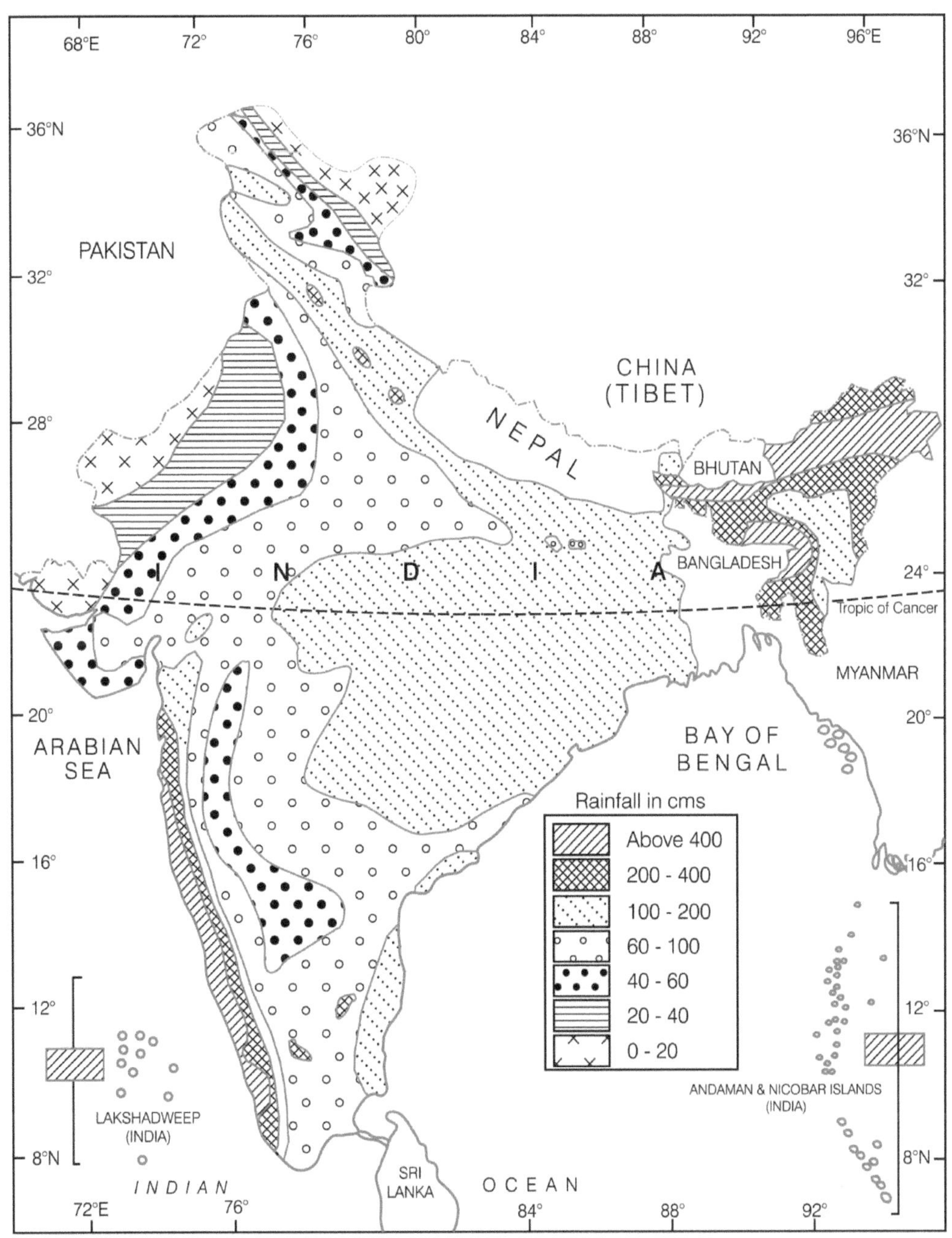

INDIA : Annual Rainfall
(Chapter-4 Climate)

This map shows the average seasonal rainfall during the period June-September (in cm) in India.

Practice Map 11

Q 11 On an outline map of India, show the following

1 Areas receiving over 400 cm rainfall
2 Areas receiving less than 20 cm rainfall.

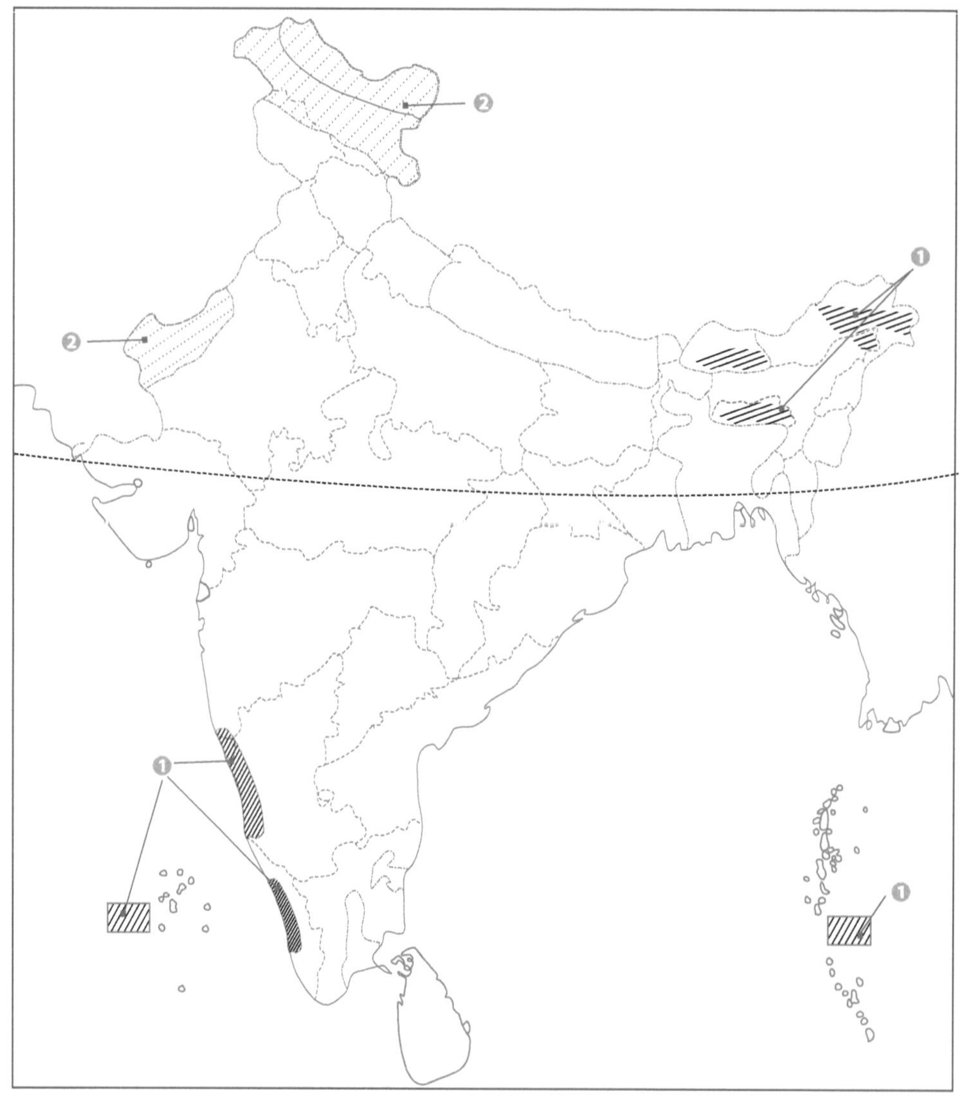

INDIA : Natural Vegetation
(Chapter-5 Natural Vegetation and Wildlife)

Natural vegetation in India includes Tropical Evergreen Forests, Tropical Deciduous Forests, Montane Forests, Mangrove Forests and Tropical Thorn Forests. This map shows the natural vegetation of India.

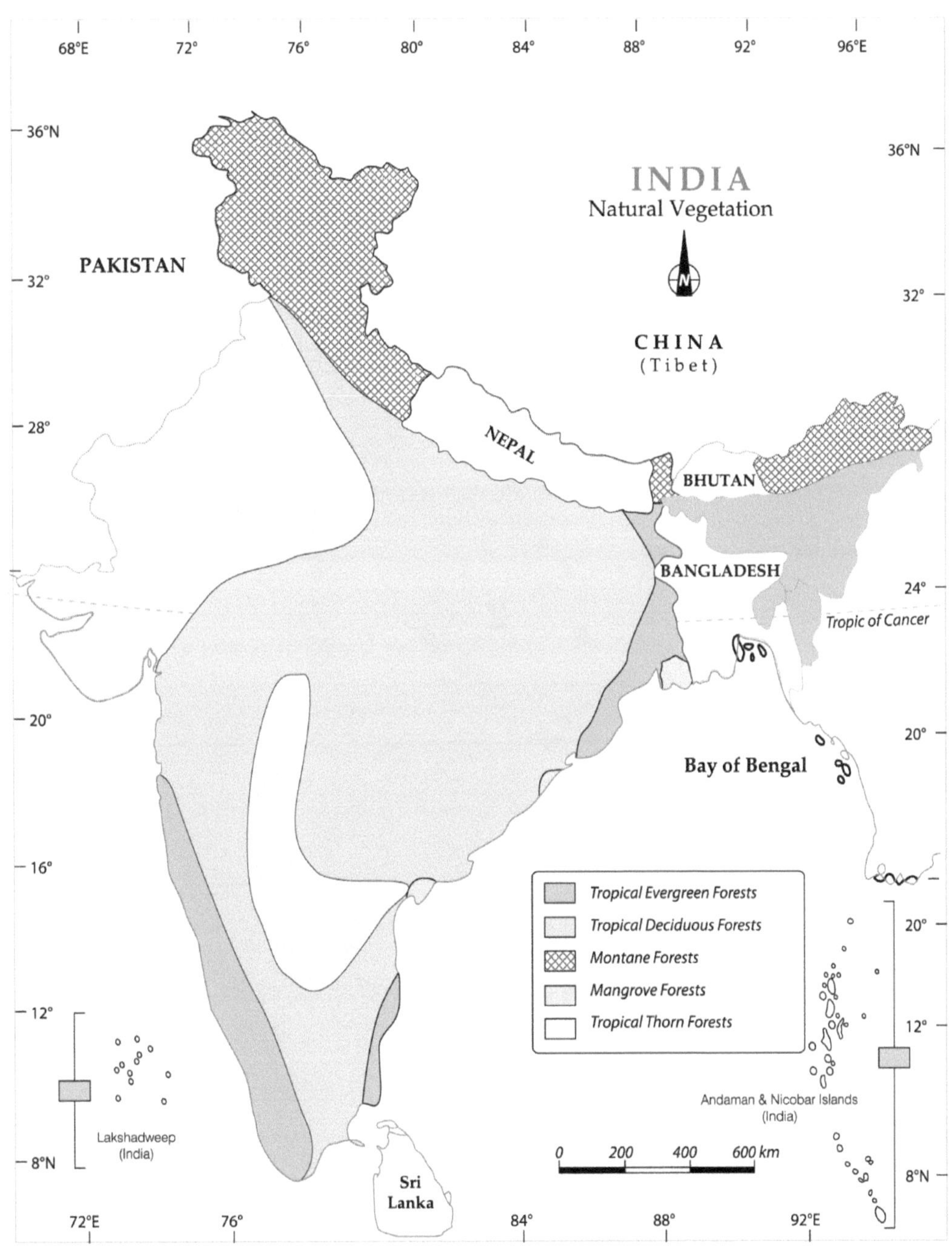

Practice Map 12

 Identify 1, 2, 3, 4 and 5 on the given map

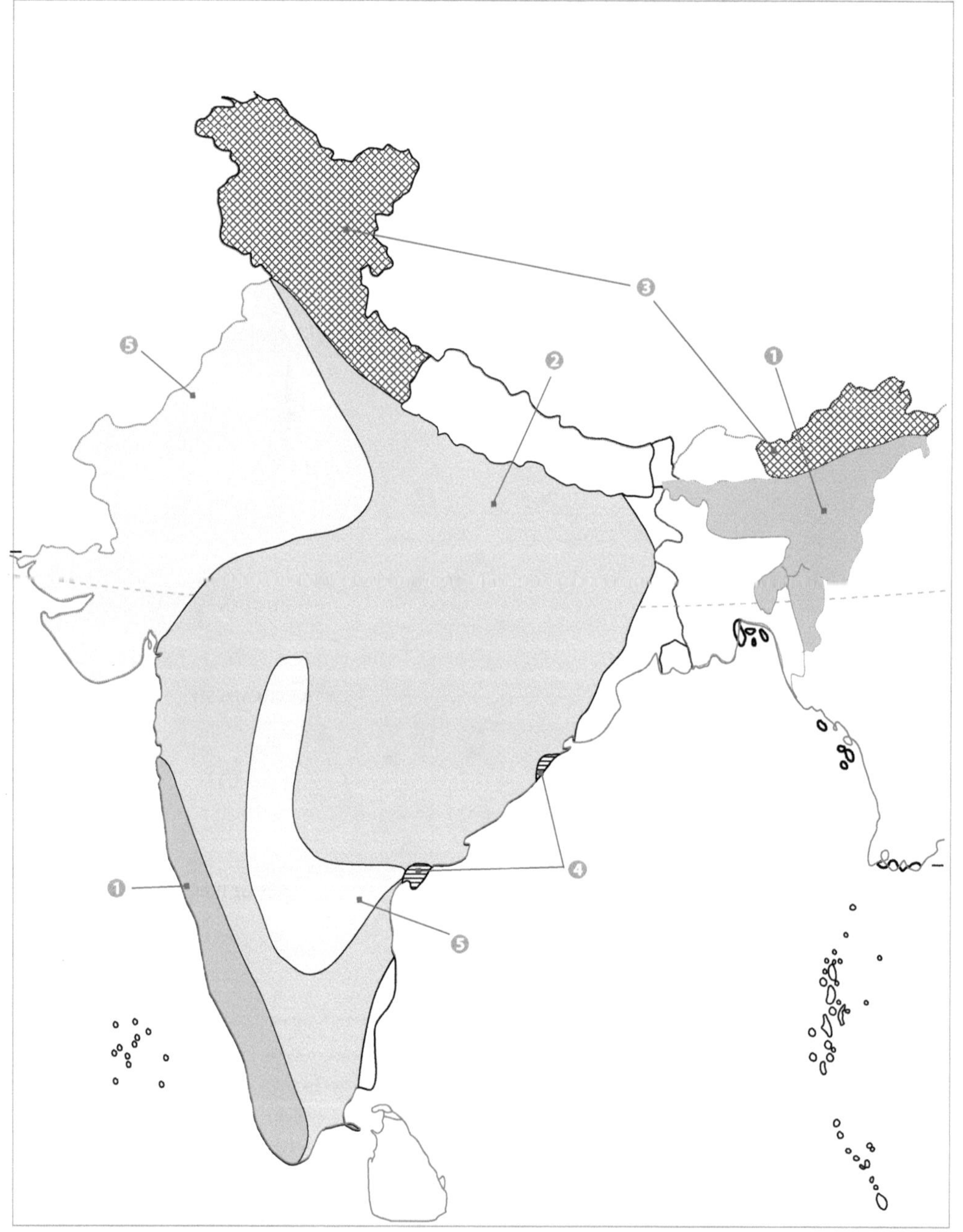

INDIA : Wildlife Sanctuaries, Bird Sanctuaries and National Parks
(Chapter-5 Natural Vegetation and Wildlife)

India is home to several fabulous wildlife sanctuaries, bird sanctuaries and national parks, which makes this country a nature lover's paradise. The map shows the major wildlife sanctuaries, bird sanctuaries and national parks of India.

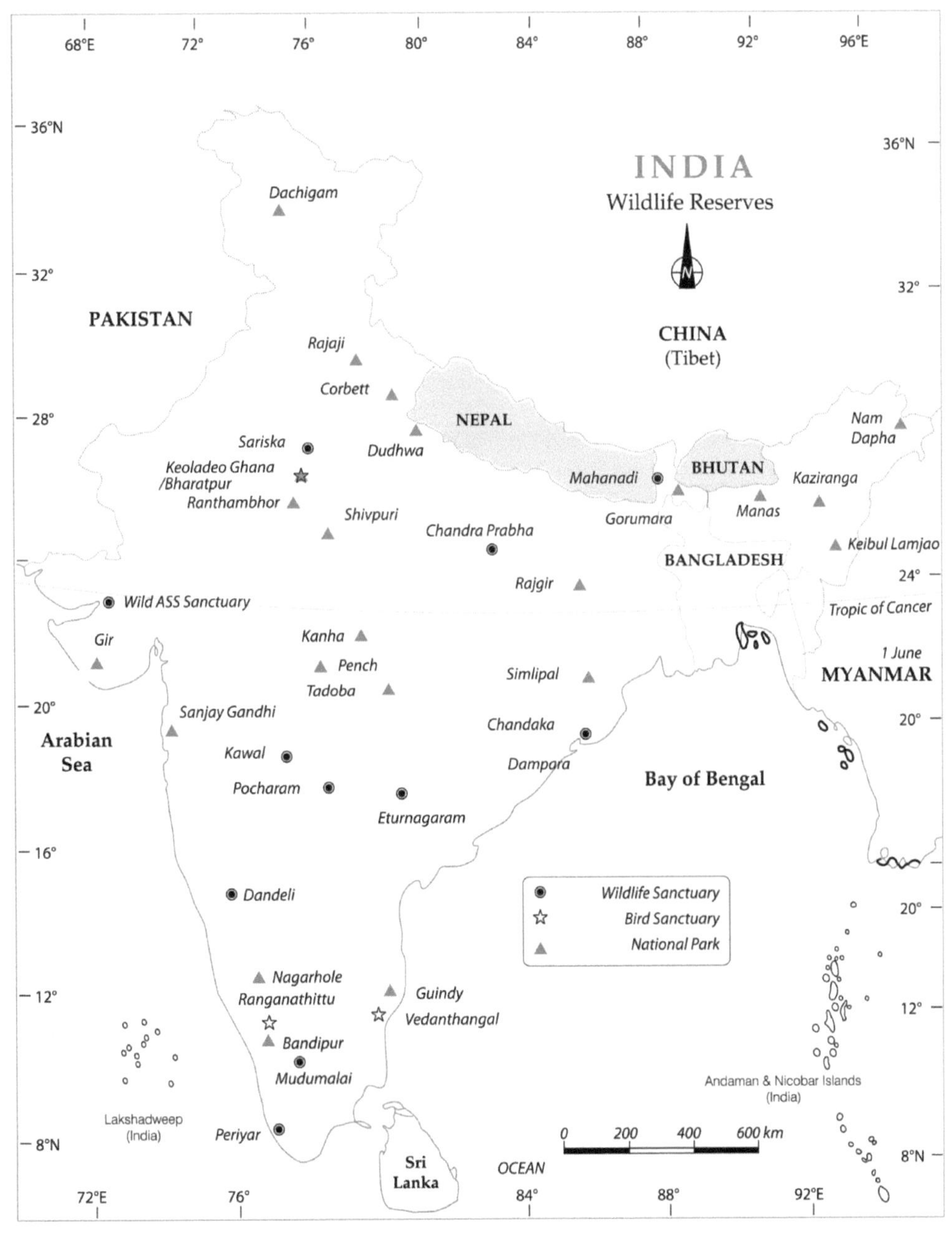

Practice Map 13

Q13 Features are marked by numbers in the given political map of India. Indentify these features with the help of the following information and write their correct names on the lines marked in the map.

1 Corbett National Park
2 Ranthambor National Park
3 Kaziranga National Park
4 Shivpuri National Park
5 Kanha National Park
6 Simlipal National Park
7 Manas National Park

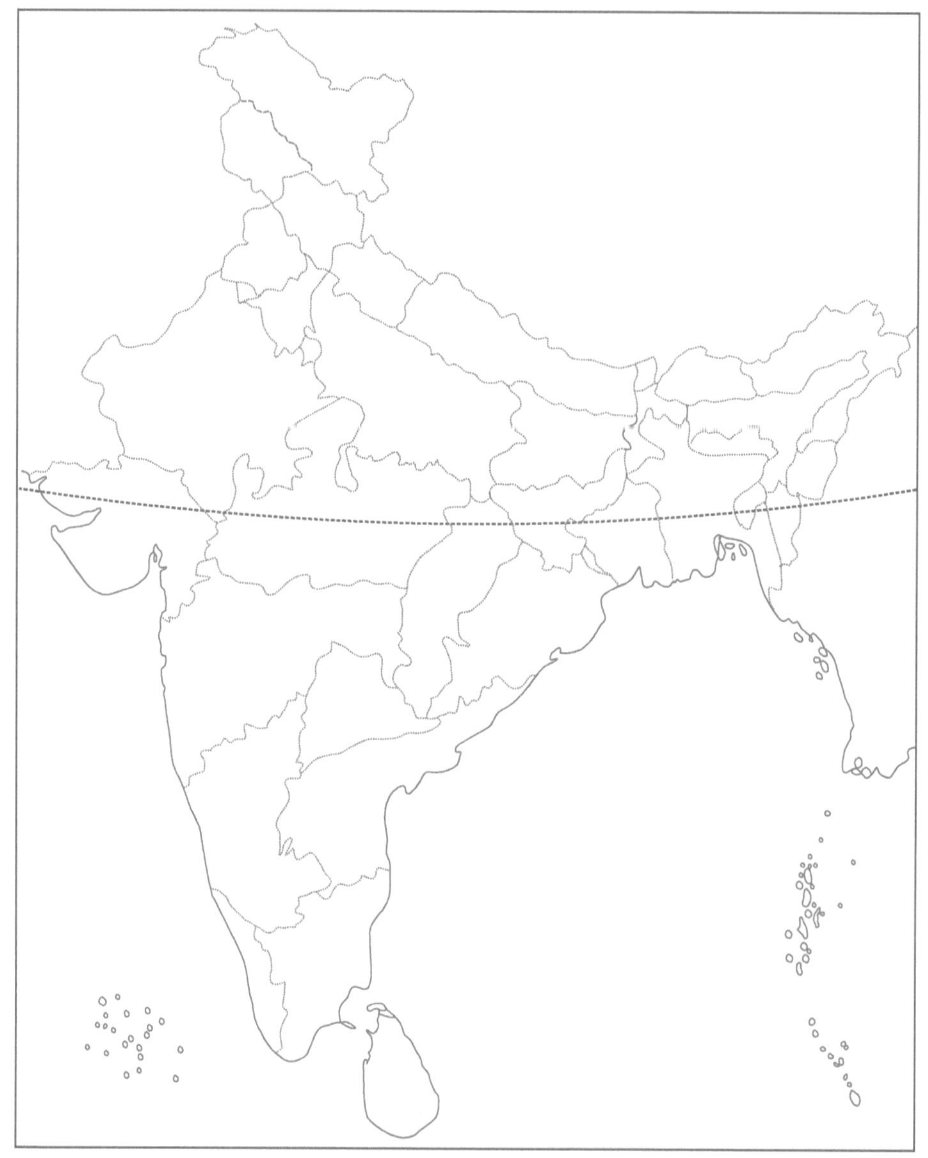

Practice Map 14

Q14 Locate and label the following items on the given map

1. Ranganathittu Bird Sanctuary.
2. Mudumalai Wildlife Sanctuary.
3. Rajaji Wildlife Sanctuary
4. Bharatpur Bird Sanctuary
5. Sariska Wildlife Sanctuary
6. Dachigam Wildlife Sanctuary

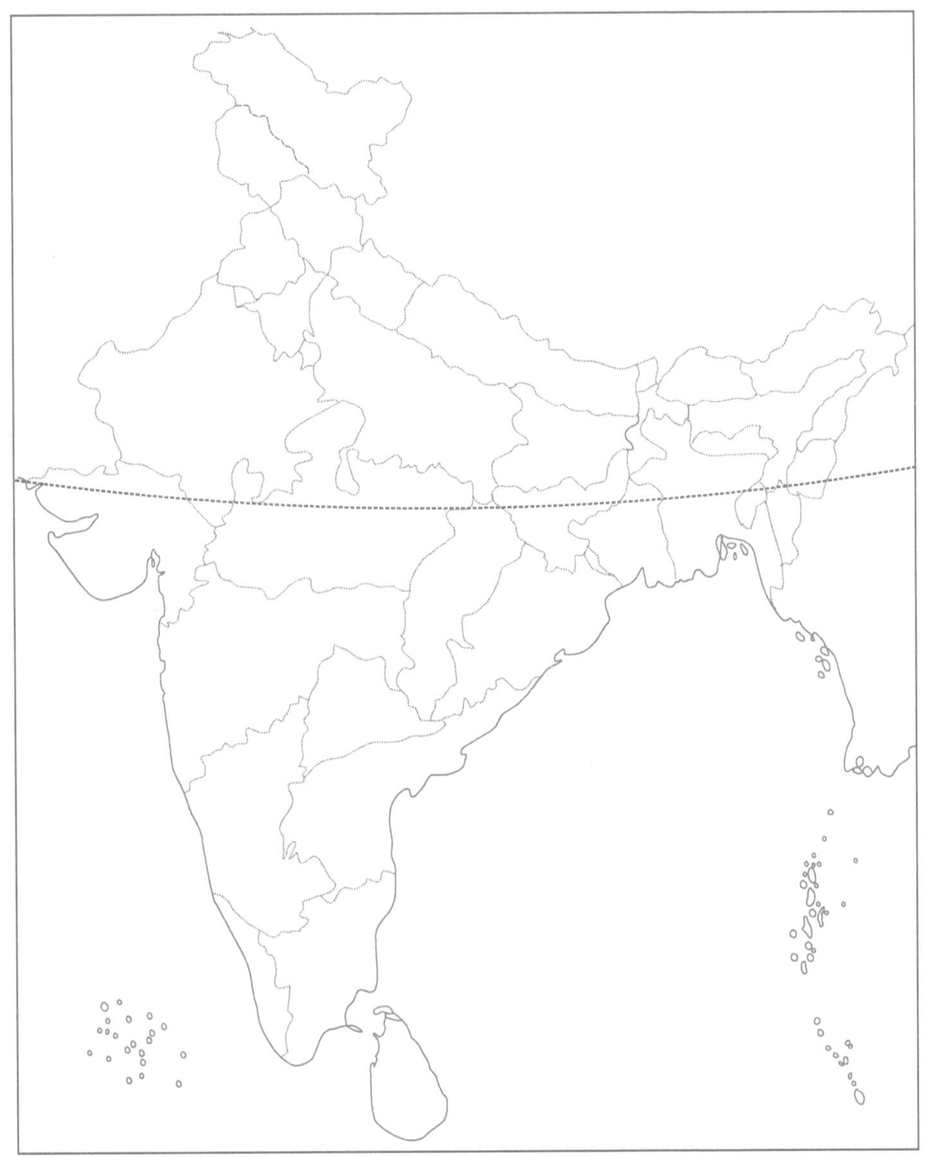

Population Density of India
(Census 2011 : Provisional Date)
(Chapter-6 Population)

In states Bihar has the highest population density, while in Union territories Delhi has the highest population density. This map shows the population density of states and Union Territories.

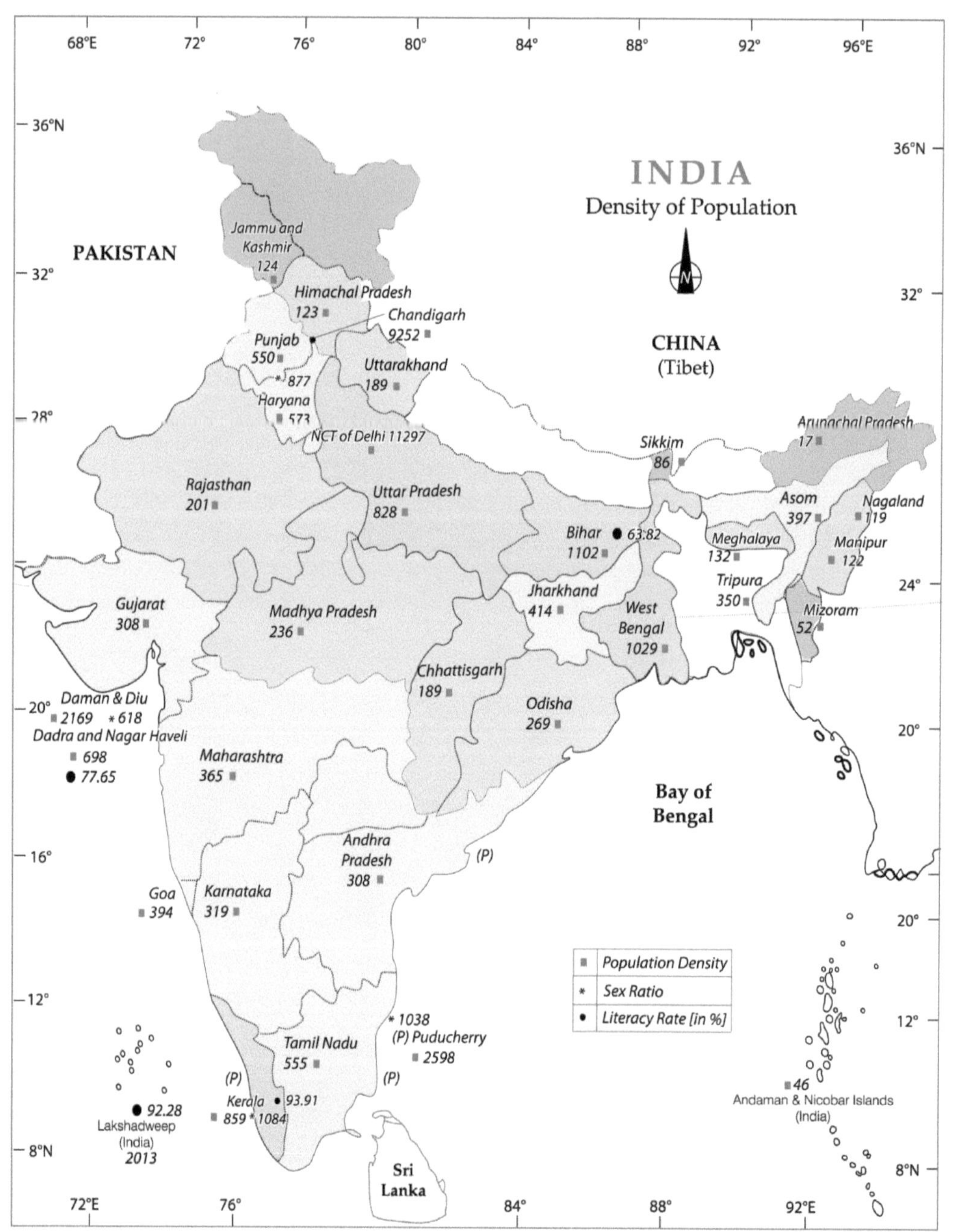

Practice Map 15

Q15 Locate and label the following items on the given map

1. The state having the highest population density.
2. The state having the lowest population density.
3. The largest state according to area.
4. The smallest state according to area.
5. The state having highest sex ratio.
6. The state with lowest sex ratio.

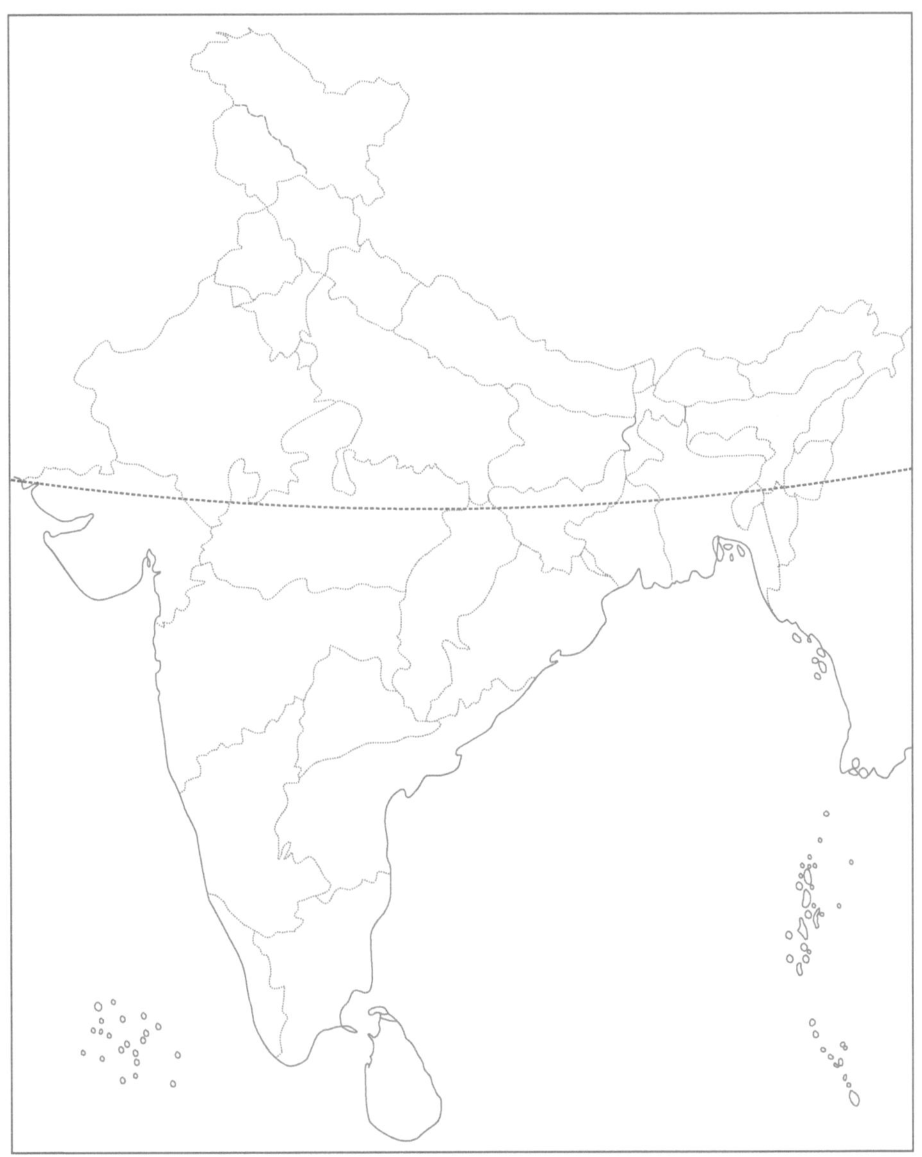

Exam Practice

Map 1

Q1 Locate and label the following item on the given political map with appropriate symbols.

   1 Western ghats

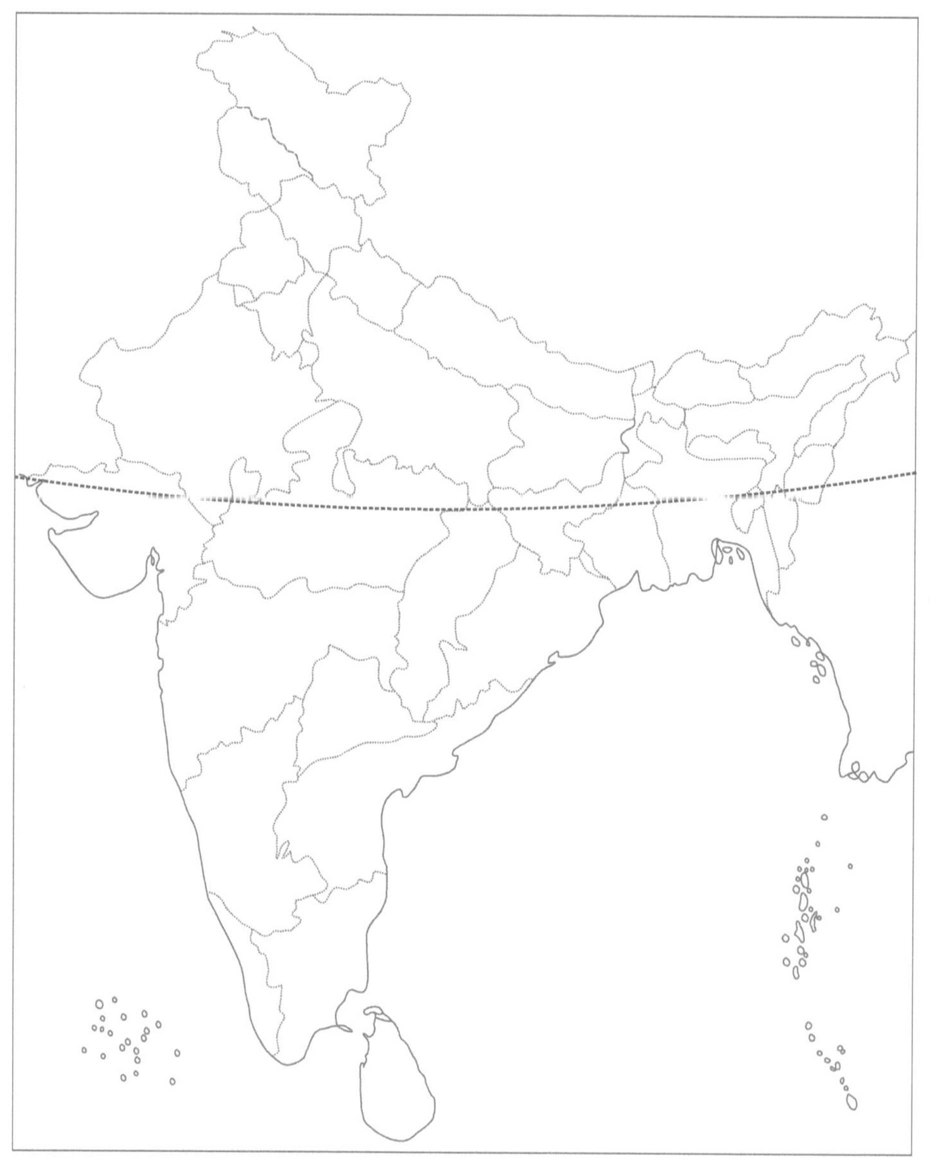

Map 2

Q2 Features are marked by number in the political map of India. Identify these features with the help of the following information and write their correct names on the lines marked in the map.

  1 A mountain range   2 A river known as Dakshin Ganga

  3 The outermost range of Himalayas

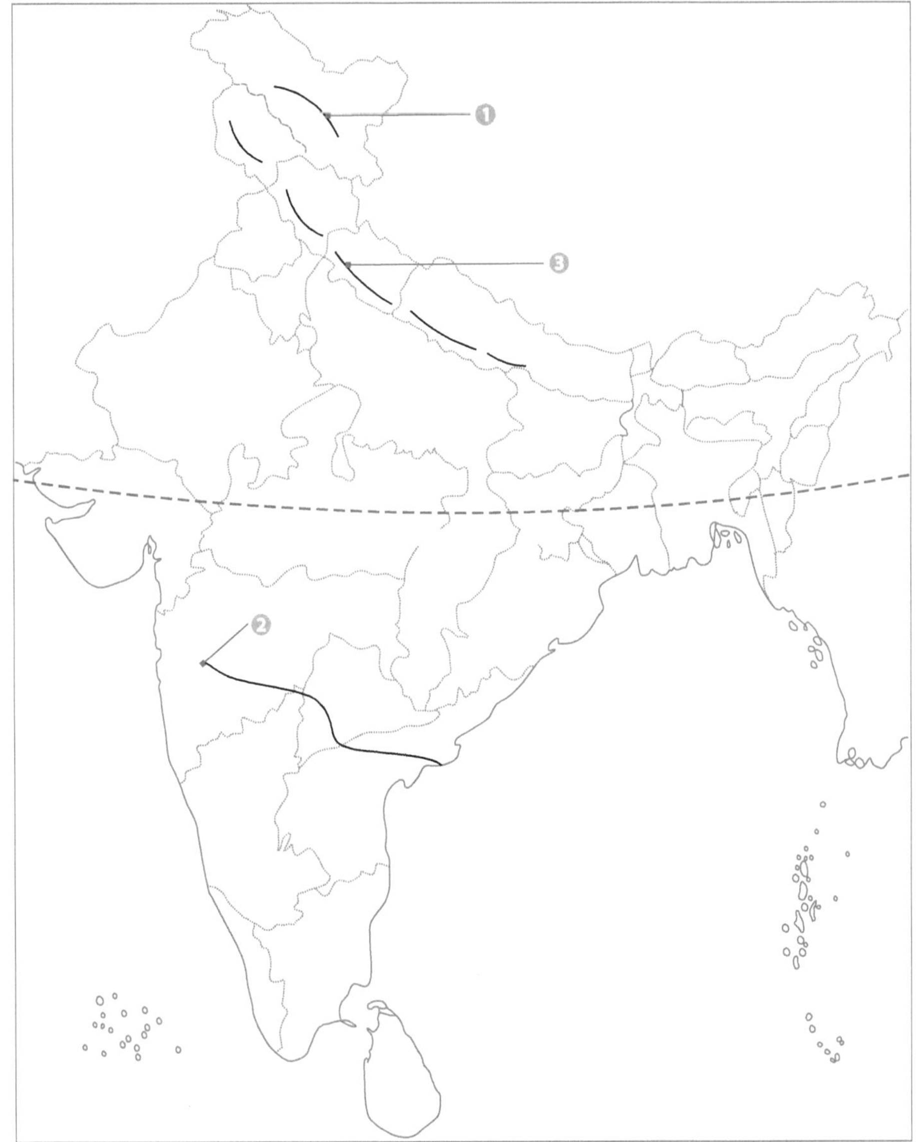

Map 3

Q3 Locate and label the following items on the given map with appropriate symbols.

1 Kanchenjunga peak

2 Eastern Ghats

3 Kaveri river

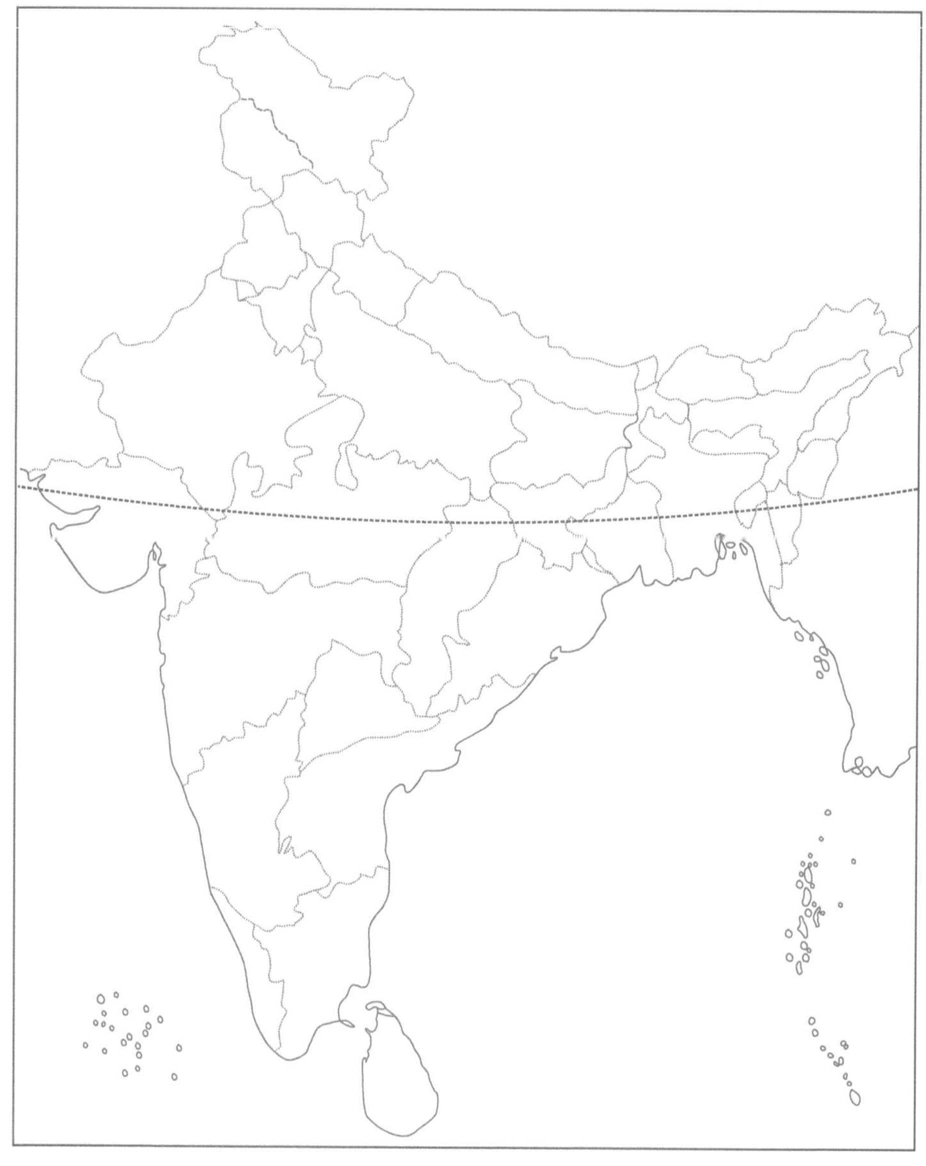

Map 4

Q4 Features are marked by numbers in the given political map of India. Identify these features with the help of the following information and write their correct names on the lines marked in the map.

1 River of Peninsular India that forms an estuary

2 A South India hill range

3 Western Coastal strip in the North

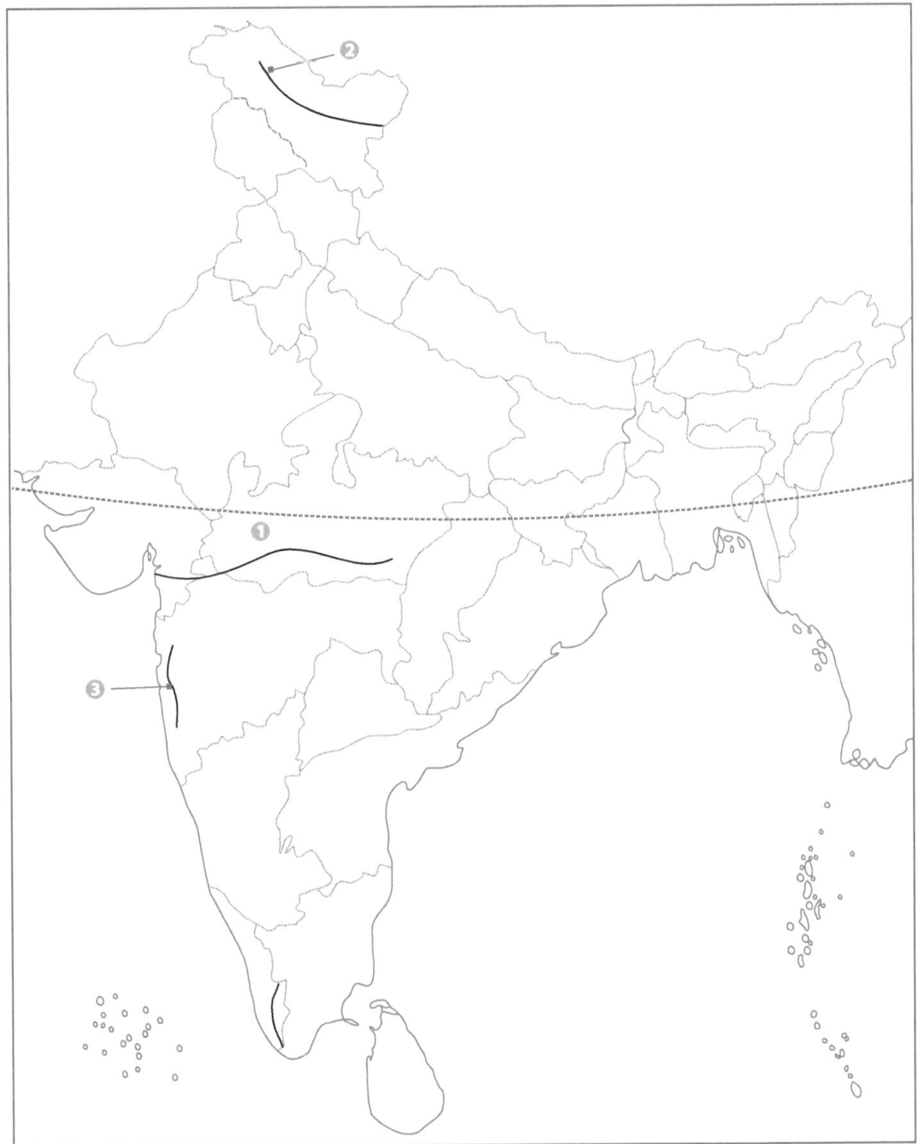

Map 5

Q5 Features are Marked by numbers in the political map of India. Identify these features with the help of the following information and write their correct names on the lines marked in the map.

    1 A National Park.

    2 National Park in Odisha.

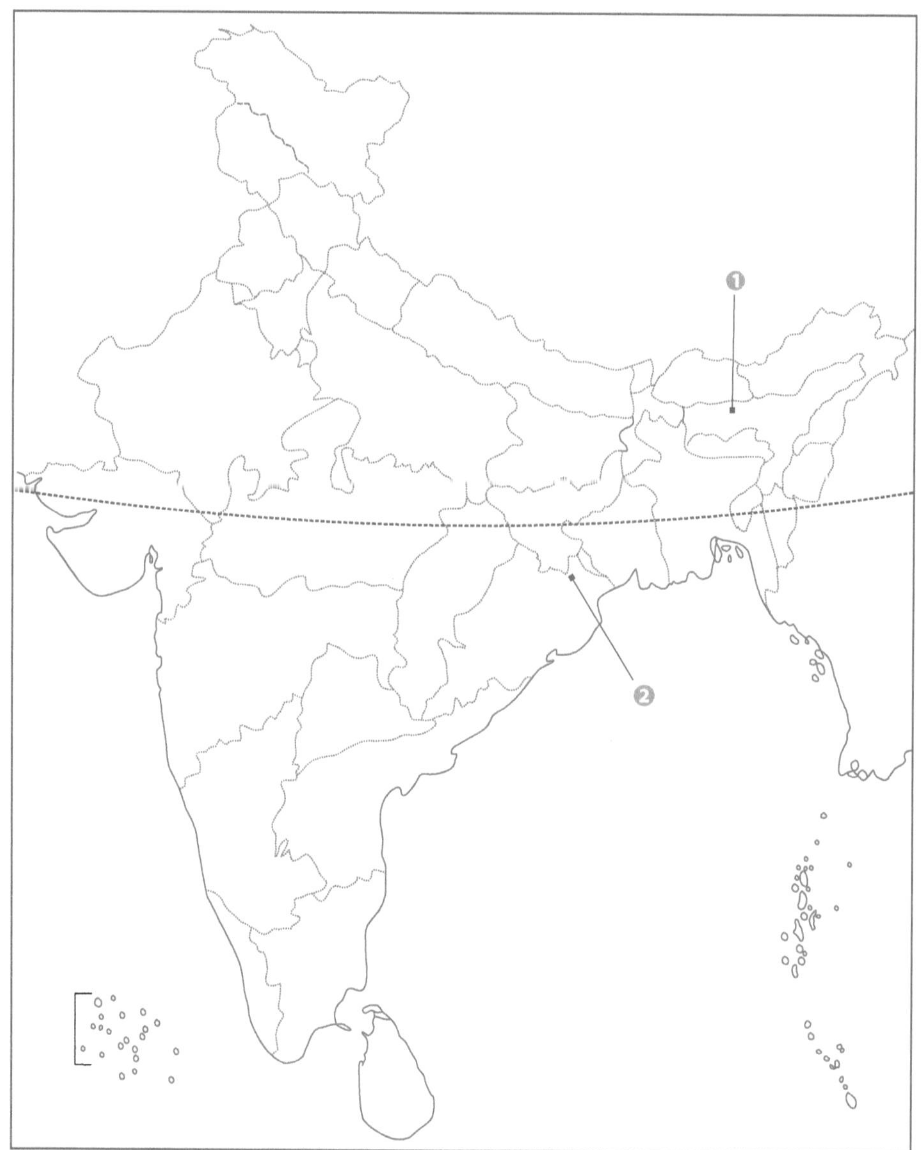

Map 6

Q6 Locate and label the following items on the given map with appropriate symbols.

1. Shivpuri National Park
2. Kanha National Park

Answers (Practice Map)

Map 1

Map 2

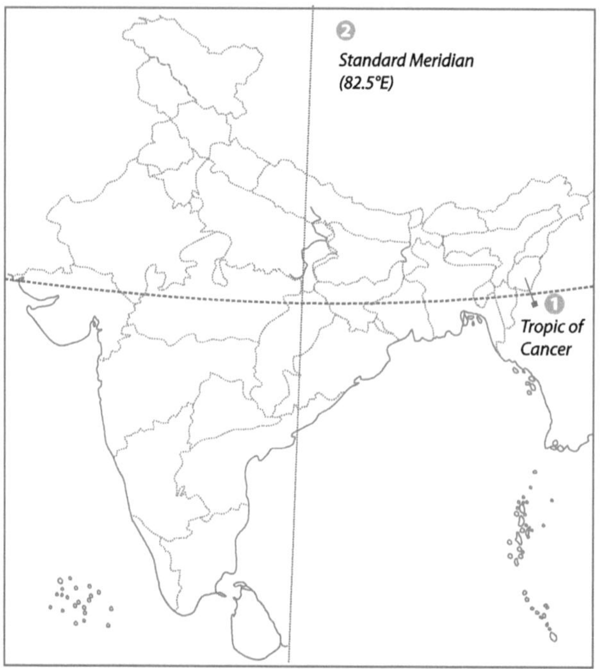

Map 3

Satpura Range
Vindhya Range
Anai Mudi

Map 4

Aravalli Range
Malwa Plateau
Chota Nagpur Plateau

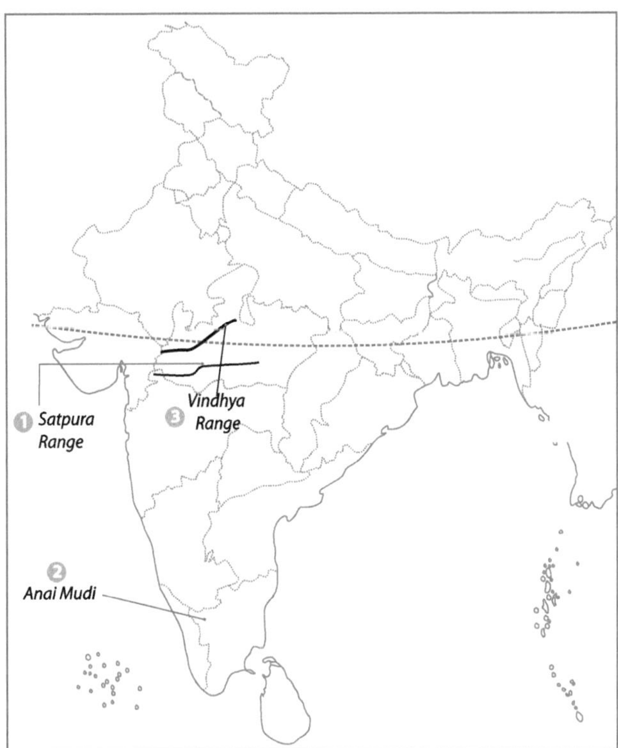

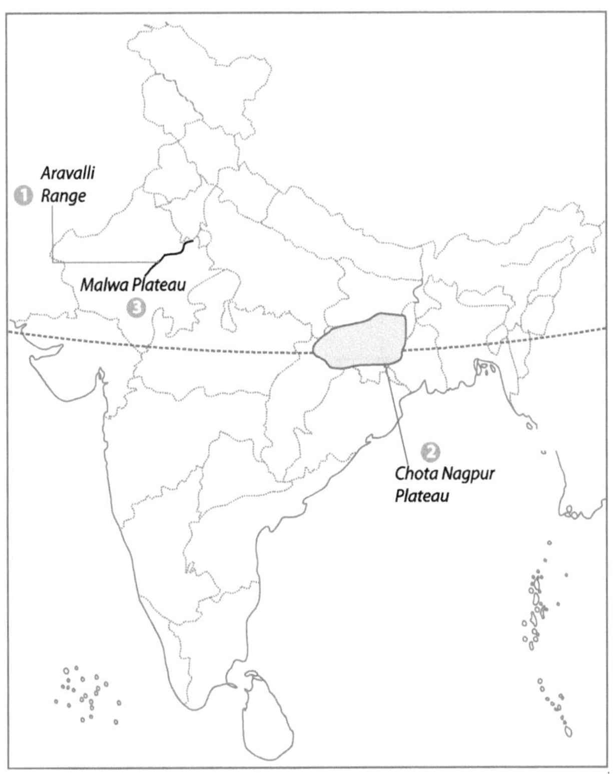

Map 5

Shiwalik Range
Kanchenjunga
Western
Ghats

Map 6

K2
Deccan Plateau
Eastern
Ghats

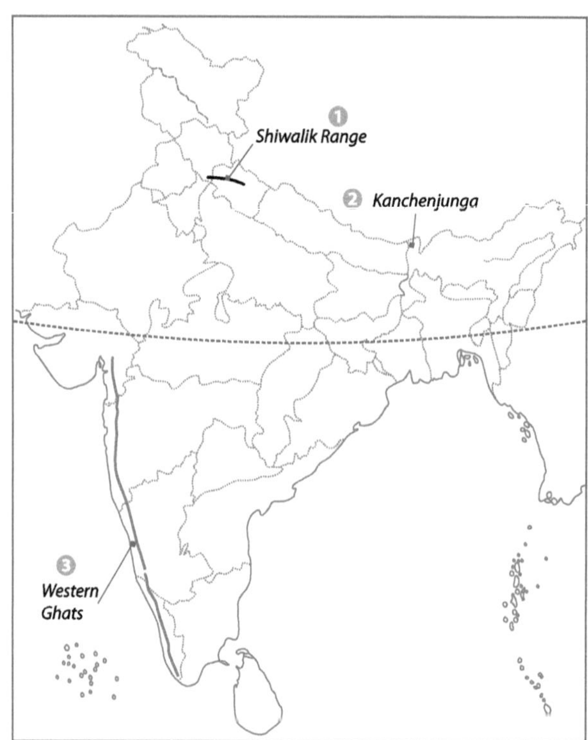

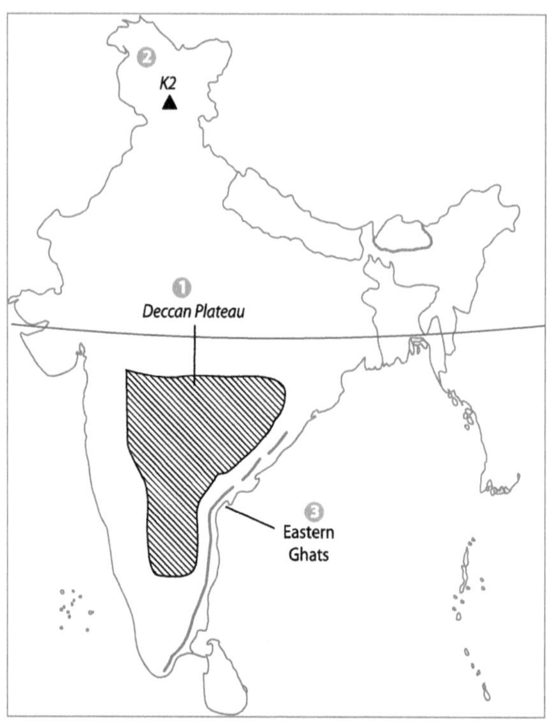

Map 7

Karakoram Range
5
6
Zaskar Range
Konkan Coast
1
Northern Circar
4
Malabar Coast
3
2
Coromandel Coast

Map 8

3
Wular lake
2
Sambhar lake
4
Chilika lake
1
Pulicat lake

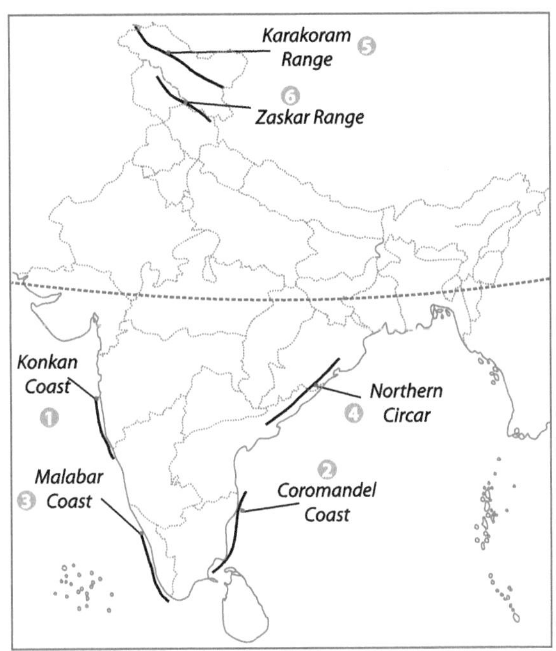

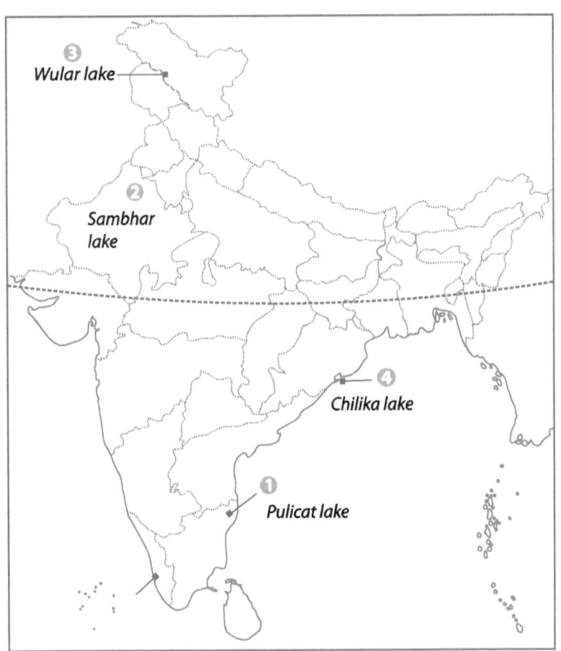

Map 9

Indus river
Satluj
Ganga

Map 10

Narmada river
Tapi river
Mahanadi river
Godavari river
Krishna river
Kaveri river

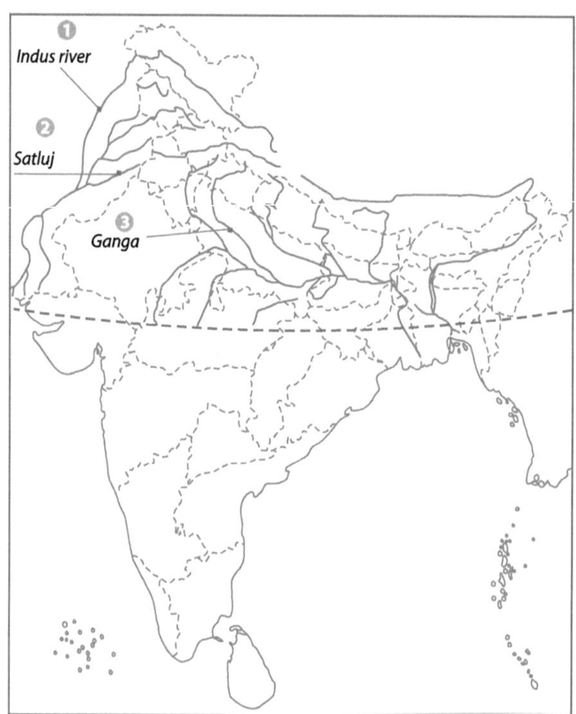

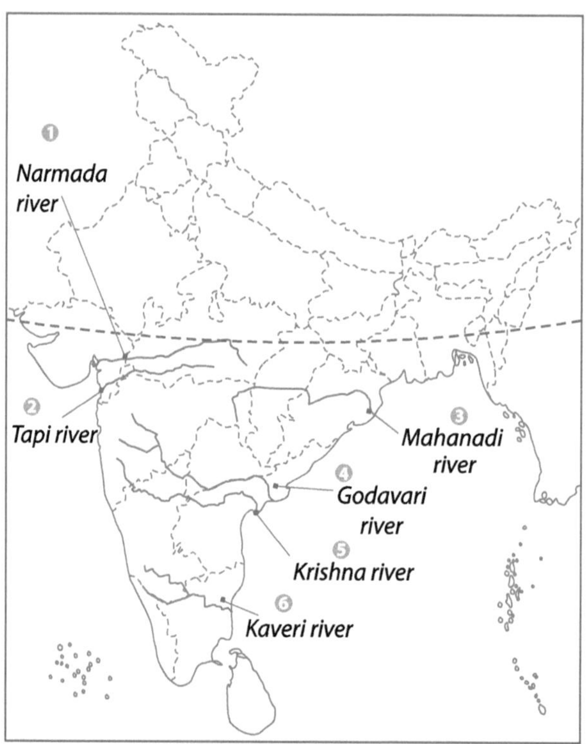

Map 11

Areas around Leh
North-eastern states
Western part of Rajasthan
Parts of Western Coast
Andaman & Nicobar Islands group
Lakshadweep

Map 12

Montane Forests
Tropical Thorn Forests
Tropical Deciduous Forests
Tropical Evergreen Forests
Mangrove Forests
Tropical Evergreen Forests
Tropical Thorn Forests

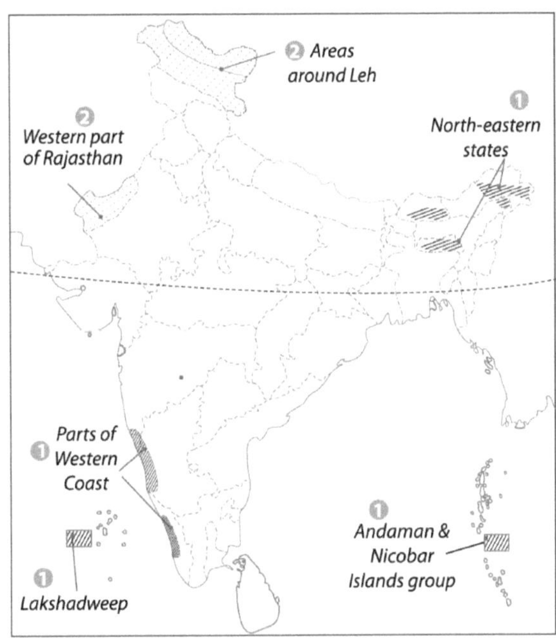

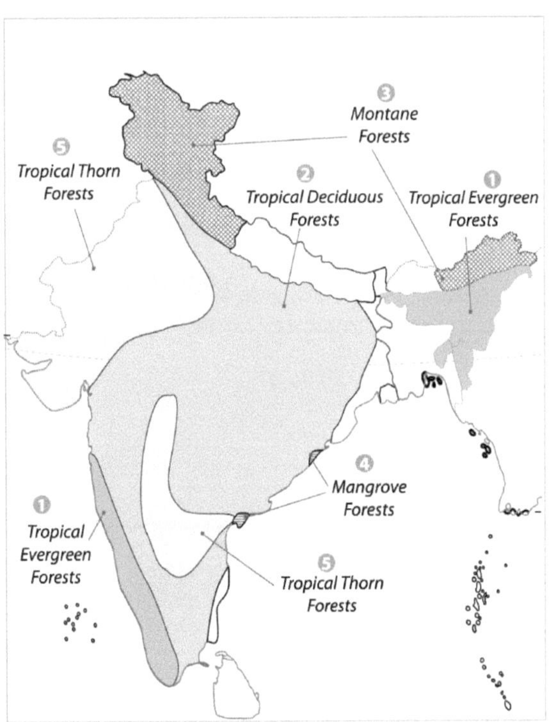

Map 13

Corbett National Park
Manas National Park
Ranthambor National Park
Kaziranga National Park
Shivpuri National Park
Simlipal National Park
Kanha National Park

Map 14

Dachigam Wildlife Sanctuary
Bharatpur Bird Sanctuary
Sariska Wildlife Sanctuary
Rajaji Wildlife Sanctuary
Ranganathittu Bird Sanctuary
Mudumalai Wildlife Sanctuary

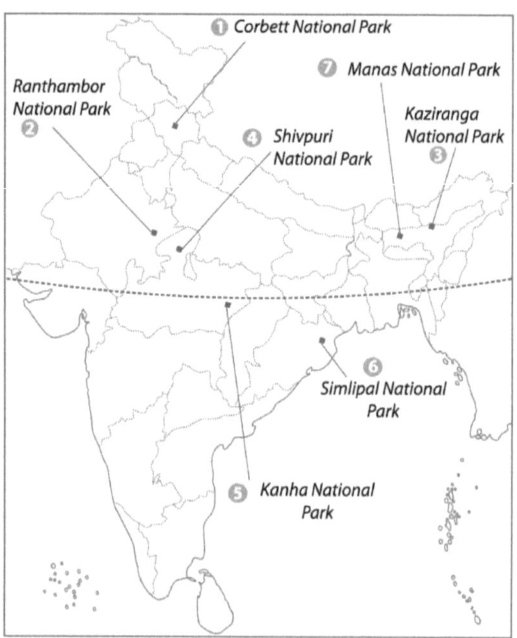

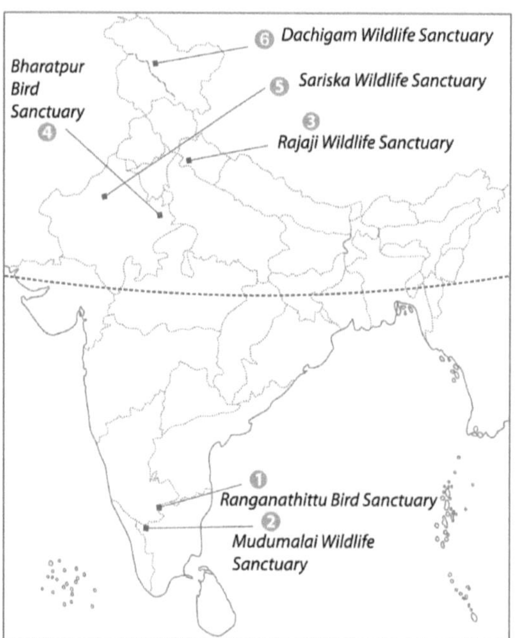

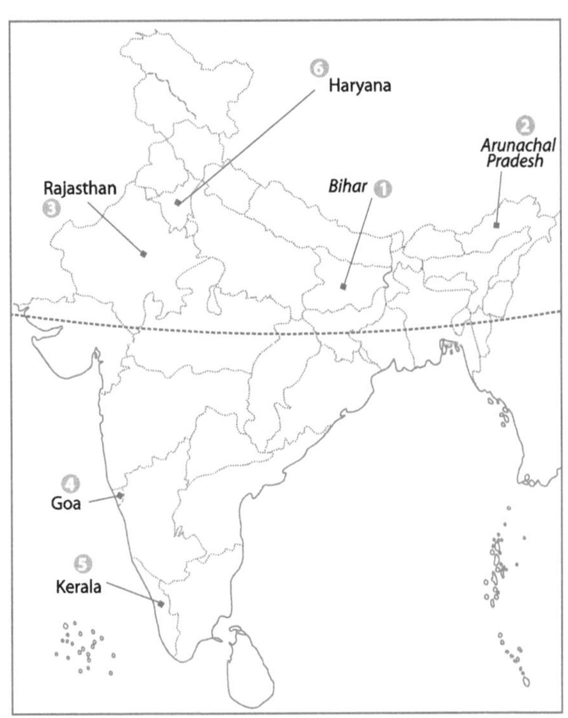

Answers (Exam Practice)

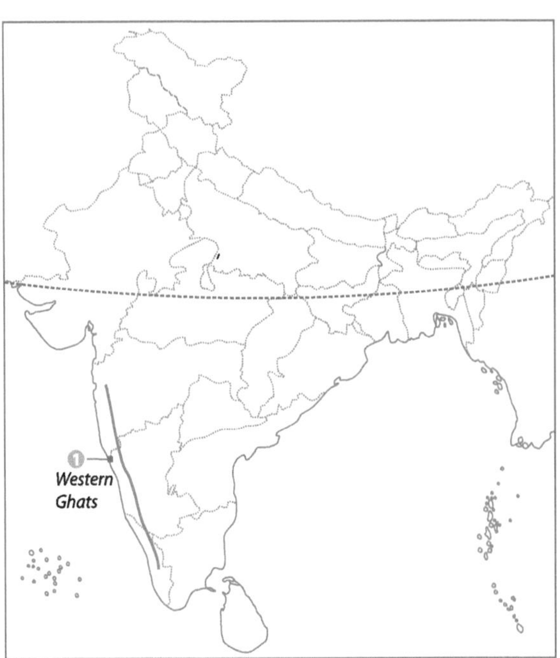

Map 2

Zaskar range
Shiwalik range
Godavari river

Map 3

Kanchenjunga peak
Eastern Ghats
Kaveri river

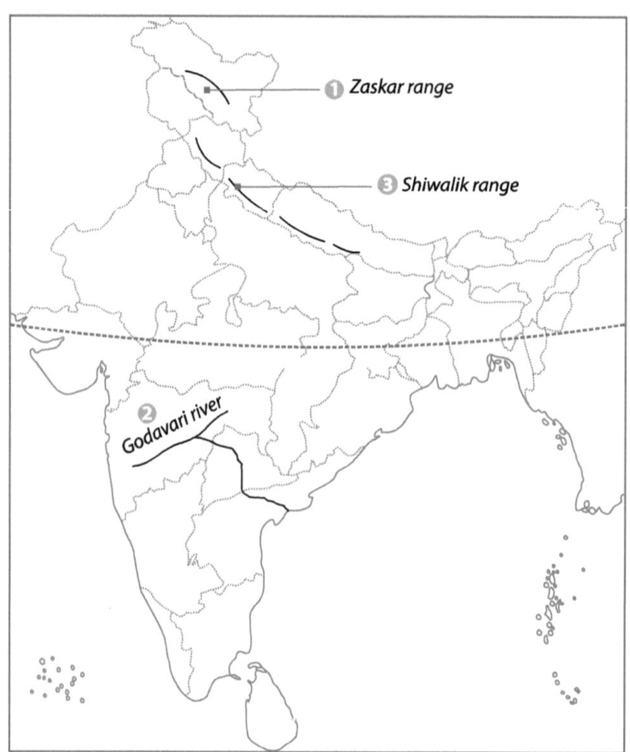

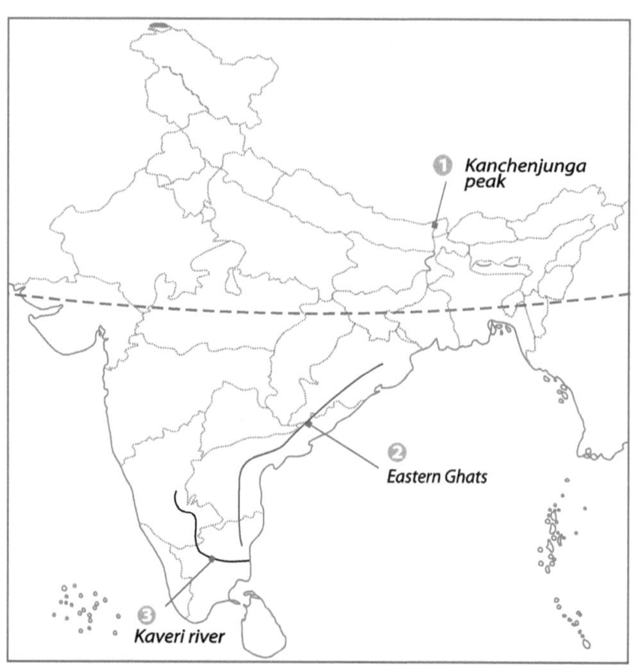

Map 4

Karakoram range
Narmada river
Konkan

Map 5

Manas National Park
Simlipal National Park

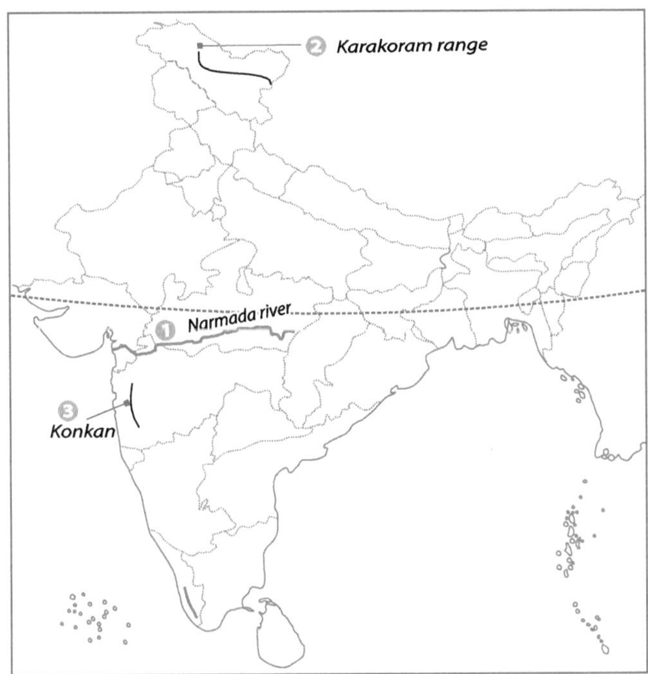

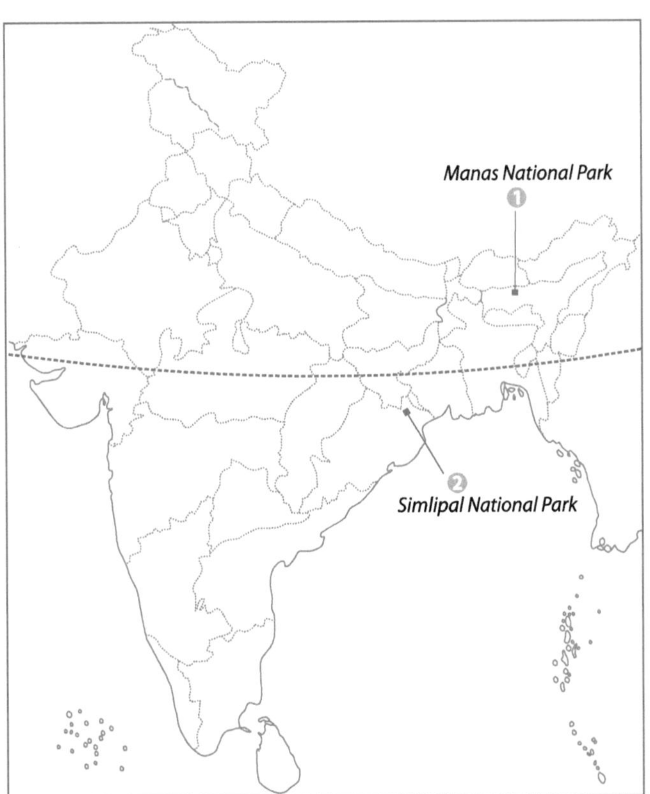

Map 6

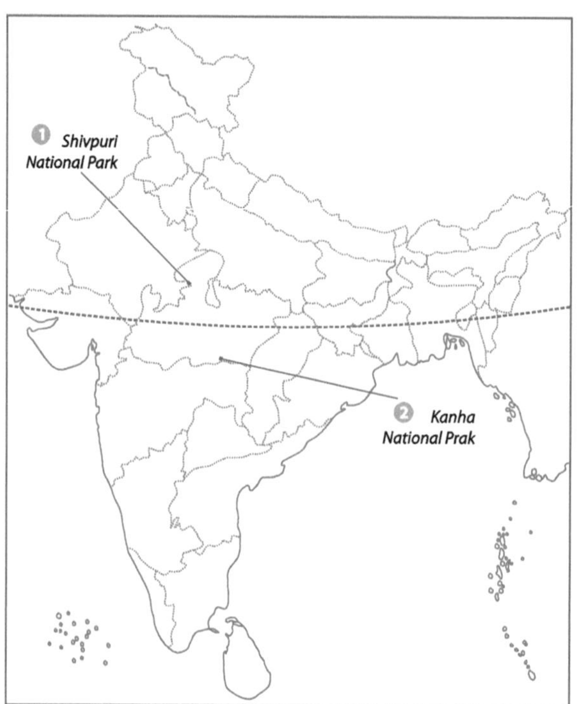

Rough Work

Rough Work

Rough Work

Rough Work

Printed by Libri Plureos GmbH in Hamburg,
Germany